WHY WAIT TO BE GREAT?

Why Wait To Be Great?
by Hayden Wilson

Published by a nice publishing co.
25 Wilson St, South Yarra, Victoria, 3141, Australia

Photography by Meagan Harding
Editing by S F Rees
ISBN: 978-0-6480966-0-3

WHY WAIT TO BE GREAT?

The Young Leader's Guide to Showing Up,
Standing Out and Shining Bright

HAYDEN WILSON

nice.

What Are The Experts Saying?

"As you enter the Temple of the Oracle at Delphi, above is written 'First Know thyself'. This is the Foundation of Personal Peak Performance. This book will help you do just that."

- Kevin Roberts, *Former CEO and Chairman of Saatchi and Saatchi, International Speaker, Consultant and Best Selling Author.*

"This book is a fantastic insight into the world of leadership and human behaviour that every individual will be enriched by reading. It will help awaken your own inspiring vision and give you the tools, confidence and attitude necessary to do what you love and love what you do."

- Dr John Demartini, *International Speaker, Best Selling Author and Founder of the Demartini Institute.*

"This is a brilliant book that will help you find your inner greatness and express it fully in the world. Make sure you read it and apply these principles as soon as possible."

- Jack Canfield, Co-author of *The Success Principles*™

To my mentors, my family, my friends and myself.
Without the above, none of this would have been possible.

Contents

Foreword

For the past 45 years, I have been researching, writing and teaching universal principles, particularly how they relate to human behaviour and maximising our full potential. Along this journey I have met and been fortunate enough to be able to assist millions of people, one of those being Hayden.

During one of my courses, he explained how he would love to write a book to help inspire the next generation of Young Leaders around the world. By the look in his eyes, I knew he was a man on a mission with an important message to share.

Then recently, after attending another of my courses, he shared with me a bound copy of the manuscript he had written since our last meeting.

As a teacher, healer and philosopher, when someone puts the principles I share into practice, I cannot help but be drawn into their vision and love to see them grow.

One of my many deeply inspiring goals is to help as many people as I can live meaningful, fulfilling and magnificent lives. I can see Hayden is doing this by stepping up and serving more people each time I see him.

This book is a fantastic insight into the world of leadership and human behaviour that every individual will be enriched by reading. It will help awaken your own inspiring vision and give you the tools, confidence and attitude necessary to do what you love and love what you do.

I am grateful to have been asked to write this introduction to this inspiring book and know when you apply the principles from within, your life will be completely transformed.

With love and wisdom
Dr John Demartini

Welcome

Ladies and gentlemen, first and foremost, I'd like to thank you for picking up this book. With the amount of information available today, it means a lot that you've chosen to invest your time in reading these words.

These days I consider myself quite lucky. Most people who see my videos, listen to my podcasts, meet me in person or read my other material might think I've always been somewhat outgoing and talkative. Then, when I tell them that just a few short years ago I was nearly the complete opposite, they can hardly believe it.

Less than half a decade ago, I was a shy, anxious, twenty-something-year-old guy who hated speaking. Not just speaking in front of crowds (a lot of people hate that), but something as simple as making a phone call would stress me to the point of paralysation.

Years of conditioning led me to believe I had nothing to say, like my voice didn't matter. I would berate myself and constantly overthink everything (and I mean *everything*). I believed my ideas were not worthy of being spoken about. I would isolate myself from situations, and my self-confidence and self-esteem were basically non-existent.

These days, things are a little different. OK, a lot different. Never in my wildest dreams did I think I would get to help Young Leaders reach their full potential through coaching, speaking from the stage, hosting life-changing events and helping them share their voice with the world.

Yet today, this is what I am fortunate enough to call my life. Like everyone, of course I have challenges, but when you can shift your thinking to see how challenges serve you, instead of hinder you, you can start to appreciate them for what they are - life's greatest teachers.

Besides, those challenges soon become a distant memory when people from all over the world send me photos, quotes, videos and screenshots of content that I have created for them. They thank me for the interviews that I have recorded with world-leading coaches. They share articles that I have written based on the 'crazy' thoughts that run through this head of mine. And they attend the events I create in order to learn from some of the world's best. It's truly humbling, and I am eternally grateful for every opportunity that has come my way - both 'good' and 'bad', because both serve.

What I have compiled for you here is a guide. A current collection of my deepest thoughts and how they can be of use for you. I can't promise that you've never heard some of this stuff, but what I can promise you is that how I share it will be new. You see, I believe we all have something to say. Like me, you have been fortunate enough to have lived through a unique set of circumstances, within a unique environment, in a unique time, with a unique bunch of people. All this uniqueness has left you with a unique story and a unique way of telling it. So *why not* share that with others?

My goal for you with this guide is not to provide earth shattering theories that require a PhD to comprehend; nor is it to regurgitate a bunch of material you can find in most modern-day self-help books. It is simply to allow you some insight into a new paradigm. My paradigm. And, of course, to share with you some of the necessary tools to bring this stuff to life and develop as a Young Leader. Before we begin, however, I have a confession to make....

I'm sorry, but I do not have all of the answers. Like you, I too am a student of the game. A lifelong learner who has dedicated his life to sharing the world's best information with the world's hungriest learners. I don't claim to be an expert, nor do I act like one. I simply strive to inspire others through action and attempt to help people live a more fulfilled life.

It does, however, raise the question: how did we get here? To be honest it was just a few years ago that I was just like 99% of the population. A mediocre kind of guy who would watch a lot of TV, was stuck in a corporate job I hated and didn't really think of anything beyond what was for dinner that night. I certainly didn't read, I certainly didn't set goals for the future and I certainly didn't think I would be writing a book.

That was until one cold winter's night at football training. One of my teammates told me about his corporate job working with a sports apparel company named 2XU. Given I already had an interest in the gym, health and fitness (and as strange as this is going to sound), I was perplexed as to how someone could work in a corporate job, but for a *fun* company. I always thought that having fun and doing what you like were completely separate from your 'work'. Yet something switched within me that night. I thought, if this guy can do it, *why can't I?*

And from that moment on, everything changed.

Within just one week, opportunities would seemingly show up out of nowhere to help guide me toward a path I never thought possible. Included in this was the fact I landed a job with one of Australia's most renowned gyms, which would see me serve an incredible apprenticeship for the next three and a half years inside the industry I love.

During that time, I discovered a man by the name of Napoleon Hill on YouTube, who shared a simple yet powerful message with me. Within just four minutes he instilled a deep confidence and inner inspiration that awoke a voice inside me who just kept repeating *Why not me? Why not me? Why not me?*

It was at this exact moment I decided I would dedicate myself to reading every book I could, travelling to every seminar I could, coaching every client I could, learning from every mentor I could and doing the work required to become better at what I love most: inspiring through action.

So while I'm certainly not a guru, my hope is that, just as Napoleon Hill did for me, I can spark some inspiration deep within you to help you develop the same mantra I carry with me to this day: *Why not me?*

As we embark on this journey together, I encourage you to open your mind, switch off from any distractions and start to write your own story.

Let's begin.

The Young Leader goes through three stages along their journey.

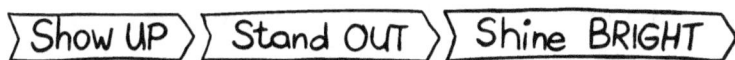

Show UP 〉 Stand OUT 〉 Shine BRIGHT 〉

This book will explore each of these 'S's' to share with you the thoughts, beliefs and actions required to continue your own journey of development as a Young Leader.

Stage 1: *Show Up*

In this section we look at what I call the heart of the leader: a new approach to taking responsibility and the keys to developing as a person of action. Next, we address your current habits and behaviours before delving into three topics seldom spoken about: preparing to embrace the confusion (you'll find no shortage of that along your journey), developing bravery and how to use the rejection you will inevitably face to propel you along your path of greatness.

Stage 2: *Stand Out*

Here I help you understand what is required to not just be in the right place at the right time, but to have the right message, attitude and underlying skills to back that message up. We start with your attitude towards learning, before jumping into the idea factory of your mind and sharing two key methodologies that will set you apart: asking for what you want and thinking differently.

Stage 3: *Shine Bright*

In this final stage I will uncover how to supercharge your efforts. I share key insights into removing your 'inner bully' before explaining how you can use your story as rocket fuel for growth. We then explore how to take massive action upon your goals while ensuring you're setting up 'soldiers' in the army of your life. I finish off by providing you with a powerful paradigm of thinking to maintain your energy throughout your leadership journey and have the biggest impact.

Throughout, there are activities and homework to complete if you wish to maximise your results. These are not compulsory, but, like anything in life, you get out what you put in...so why not try?

The road to becoming a Young Leader is not an easy one. It will be riddled with uncertainty, self-doubt, deep worry and moments filled with anxiety. I can guarantee that, at times, you're going to want to give up; however, it's the resilience, grit and downright mental fortitude you're going to develop along this path that soon become your reward. The knowing that who you are today, as you read this page, is not the person you will be tomorrow, or the next day or in twelve months' time. If you're prepared to make that leap and ready to develop into your best you, turn the page and let's begin our time together.

PART 1: SHOW UP

Woody Allen once wrote "80% of success is showing up". Couldn't be more true. By picking up this book, you're showing me something. Something important. Maybe you're dissatisfied with your current life and thinking *there's got to be more than this?* Maybe you're not where you want to be, or you thought you'd be further ahead than this by now? Or maybe you're just looking for another way of living to supercharge things? In any case, by holding this book and reading these words, you're showing me that not only are you in the top percentile of young people who want to learn, lead, love and live their life to the fullest, but also that you are *lucky*. I'm the first to admit luck and success don't have a lot in common, but…

You have *eyesight* to read these words, *hands* to hold these pages, *clothes* on your back, a *roof* over your head and, above all, the ability to *choose*. You can choose what you read, listen to, watch and, for the most part, do. Many do not have this privilege. So congratulations on not only showing up, but also being in the right place at the right time with the right book.

We begin our journey by exploring what is at the core of any good leader. A specific set of skills and traits that you, as a Young Leader, will need to develop along your path.

The Heart of the Leader

At our core, I believe we are all leaders. It's just some have learned how to share that more effectively than others. When we know our purpose, values and underlying drivers, we are able to unleash our inner leader. From the hundreds of books I have read, thousands of interactions I have been involved in and countless conversations I have had with people from all walks of life, young and old, rich and poor, very fortunate and less fortunate, there are some common themes, behaviours and traits to be seen. These sit at what I call the 'heart of the leader'. The list below is not exhaustive, but, instead, my interpretation of what is at the core of any good leader. As you read through, take a mental note of which you currently possess and which you need to develop.

1. Lead, Don't Manage

In 2014, I was thrown into a management position that I wasn't ready or prepared for. They say when put into a situation like that, you either sink or swim. I sank. Instead of listening, I attempted to dictate the rules. Instead of communicating directly, I would leave notes. Instead of learning about my new team, I focused on myself and my goals. I was a terrible manager. I wish I'd known what I know now. Things would be a lot different. Nowadays I am *obsessed* with leadership. I read about it, I learn about it, I teach it, I speak it and, most importantly, I live it. This is the only way forward. We must all learn to lead. No matter what age, or level of experience, leadership is the answer. The question I have for you is: are you ready to become obsessed with leadership too?

2. Ability to Put Yourself in *Their* Shoes

But alone, simply giving yourself the title of leadership is not enough. To truly call yourself a leader, you'll need to also possess the key skills that lie within authentic leadership. At the top of this list sits empathy for others.

There's a great quote many sales trainers use: "If you can see yourself through John Smith's eyes, you can sell John Smith what John Smith buys". Doesn't just make sense in sales though - it makes sense in life. The Young Leader understands that to truly understand someone, they must remove all judgement. They cannot form biased opinions, nor listen to hearsay. They must remain objective and see things for what they are. Young Leaders listen, hard. They're prepared to get their hands dirty and would never ask someone to do something they themselves wouldn't do. Your job as a leader is to step into the shoes of those you lead, help guide them to the best outcome and, together, achieve more.

3. Communication is a Two-Way Street

Once you've developed an awareness of empathy, we will need to open the conversation. It is said the key to human communication is not to act interesting, but, instead, to be interested. Yet most do not. Most are simply waiting for you to stop speaking to claim their turn to talk. That's not communication. To really communicate, you need to listen as well. It's a two-way street. When I began to harness this approach and truly started listening to others, I found just how interesting the world really is. I got to know people I never knew. I understood what people were thinking. I learned that everyone has a story to tell and that everyone wears a sign around their neck stating 'I am important'. Best of all, I learned that as a leader, it was part of my job to honour this and help people be heard. H. Jackson Brown Jr once wrote "everyone you meet is afraid of something, loves something and has lost something". One of my favourite quotes. Never judge, always stay open and listen twice as much as you speak. You'll be surprised at just how much you can learn and what doors will open for you.

4. Think for Yourself

But rookies beware: unless you're developing your own thoughts and thinking for yourself, you will never be a leader. All leaders are learners, and while effective learning is an essential part of your journey, along the way you'll need to also develop your critical thinking muscle. Effective learning is not simply acting as a sponge and taking in everything that is said without careful consideration, but, instead, ingesting information through your own filter. Every single day we are exposed to thousands upon thousands of messages. If we took in everything we heard, saw or experienced, our brains simply could not cope with the constant influx. Instead, we need to switch on our filter and *decide* what is important (and what is not). I encourage all Young Leaders to listen to everything, while listening to nothing. You need to form your own opinions. To have the ability to take on new information, run it through your filter and decide for yourself *is that for me?*

No matter what the book, self-development programme or seminar, you need to have this filter switched on. No-one has all the answers. Not Tony Robbins. Not Dr John Demartini. Not Robin Sharma. Despite doing some pretty remarkable things, at the end of the day they're just people like you and me. They've just learned a specific formula for life, and they live true to it every day. It works for them, and it's inspiring to watch them live in their greatness, but what works for them might not work for you. Now it's your turn. You need to find what works for you and flex that thinking muscle. "Education is not the learning of facts, but the training of the mind to think" - Albert Einstein.

5. Courage to Show Up

But what do we do when fear rears its ugly head? This certain reality demands we have an approach that will not just help us stand up to the fear, but one that allows us to blast through the other side of our self-made walls and emerge even stronger.

I liken the job of a leader to that of someone walking into a dark cave, carrying nothing but a stick lit by a flame. Behind is a tribe relying on their leader's guidance for a greater future. Even though the leader is faced with the daunting task of entering an unknown environment with nothing but uncertainty ahead, they do it because they know that if they don't, the consequences may be deadly. Without this leadership and guidance, the entire tribe's survival is in jeopardy. It's in these situations that the leader needs to muster up all the courage they can. Yes, it's scary, and yes, it's difficult, but nobody said it was going to be easy. Go ahead and take the plunge. I promise it will be worth it.

6. Inspire Through Action

If only everyone knew what comes after the fear, though. Liberation, freedom and a no-limits attitude. There are two routes to success. The first - find someone who has done what you want to do and follow their path. The second - be the first. In either case, action is required. Nothing is more inspiring than seeing someone act upon their dreams and achieve big by putting in the work.

Thing is, I can sit here all day and share with you the leadership wisdom that I have learned, but unless you see me live it, you're not going to pay much attention. The best leaders do what they say they'll do, when they said they'll do it.

How many times do we hear so-called gurus speak about the importance of diet and exercise, only to head straight for the buffet at lunch to woof down some sandwiches? Despite the known health dangers, how many times do we see doctors smoking? When the video doesn't match the audio, you're *out of sync*. I live my life as if at any point a photographer could snap a picture of me and put it on the front page of the newspaper. When you do what you say and always strive to inspire through your actions, your role as a leader becomes a lot clearer to those watching.

7. Stick to Your Truth

Lastly, none of this will be possible without honouring your own personal values set within. Deep inside us all, we have a unique set of personal values that determine how we think, behave, decide upon things and ultimately act. We love learning around these areas, and we invest our time and money to improve them. Our conversations gravitate towards them and if we are lucky, our career will be based around them too. It's our internal compass that allows us to separate right from wrong and good from bad. Thing is, anyone can act bold while things are smooth. It's when our values are challenged that we need to draw power from within. With so many people offering their opinion on how you should run your life, this is often challenging.

Being a leader requires you to do things that have never been done before. That means at times you'll need to stand out on the edge of life where you are vulnerable and open to attack, and place your reputation on the line. This not only requires the courage and tenacity to keep going when you have no idea if things are going to work, but also the ability to keep a brave face in front of those you're leading.

You're going to need to constantly be on the lookout for smarter, more efficient ways to achieve a goal. For some, that is motivating; for others, it makes them want to curl up and disappear. Leadership is your opportunity to stand up and be great. Most miss this opportunity, though. Paraphrasing Thomas Edison, it's probably because "opportunity is dressed in overalls and looks a lot like hard work". The Young Leader understands this and, instead of complaining, shying away from the challenge or retreating to safety, they see it as an opportunity for growth. So roll up your sleeves, prepare to get your hands dirty and let's get busy sculpting you into the Young Leader you were destined to be.

Getting YOU Right

Before we jump headfirst into the lifelong journey we call leadership, however, we need to focus on the one thing underpinning it all - *you*. In order to effectively lead others, first, we must learn to lead ourselves. At its core, all leadership is self-leadership. We are all our own biggest project.

Become the CEO of your Life

I want you to imagine you're the CEO of 'Business You'. Inside this business there are several different divisions. A finance division, a social club, a health and wellness division, a research and development division, internal and external relations and overall direction. Each has its own manager, who is in charge of producing results, and a team of workers responsible for doing the work.

If someone were to perform an audit of these departments right now, what would they discover? Is 'Business You' running at a profit or a loss? That is, are you feeling fulfilled or is your life constantly feeling like a struggle? As the CEO of 'Business You', you need to be meeting regularly with all departments and understanding the various programmes running in your life. You need to know what's working, what's not and how to bring in the necessary help to get things back on track. While most wait for someone else to take care of the most important elements of their lives, the Young Leader takes control.

Direction

Who's driving the ship? Do you have direction? Where will 'Business You' be in 12 months? Five years? Twenty-five years? Is everyone on the same page? Are there regular meetings for reviewing the current direction and also future planning? If things continue the way they're currently heading, what will the outcome be? And is that what you want?

Finance Department

How are you financially? Does your Finance Manager have control of things? Aware of all incomings, outgoings and additional expenses? On top of what needs to be put away for taxes, savings and daily operations? Or are they recklessly spending with no regard for the future? How much money is required to live and grow? What about long-term sustainability? Is your company in debt or in a healthy financial position?

The Social Club

How about the social club? Are there regular outings and interactions as a part of your business? What is being performed on a monthly, weekly and daily basis to keep social engagement high inside 'Business You'? What are the business' hobbies? Are there members of the club that need to be let go and others that need to be recruited? Fun is the lifeblood of a successful life. Make sure you're having enough of it. Focus on providing extraordinary experiences, and draw in the energy required.

Research and Development

Is your R&D department on top of new trends? How is their knowledge of best practice? Does the manager read? Take courses? Listen to podcasts and audiobooks? Watch inspirational and insightful material? 'Business You' will need to develop a lifelong learning programme with a focus on continuous improvement to ensure it's constantly evolving.

Health and Wellness Programme

What about the health and wellness programme you run internally? As you get busier and busier, are you letting your health slip or does it maintain its status among the top priorities? A healthy workforce is a productive workforce. Are your employees getting adequate rest? Eating a healthy and nutritious diet? Or is your department manager fuelling your team with junk? Remember, garbage in, garbage out. Stay on top of your health. Stress, rest, renew. (We'll learn more about this one a little later on.)

Relations

What about the relations as a part of your company - both internal and external? Is your partner supporting the business or hindering it? What needs improvement? Is it giving to others or simply taking? And as the CEO, are you spending time developing relationships or are you simply waiting for *someone else* to do it for you? Step up and take control.

While most have no idea what is happening on the ground floor of their company, the best leaders have visibility at all times. At the ground level, they know the ins and outs of each department and programme. They have systems in place and protocols to run. Instead of sitting in their closed-off offices with zero visibility over the real workings of the business, they're in control and constantly looking at ways to improve.

To succeed, you need to care about 'Business You'. Let me ask: do you truly care? Would you hire you? Perform an audit today and discover what needs improvement. Do not stick your head in the sand and hope for the best - if you need help, ask for it.

Taking FULL Responsibility

At the peak of this mountain top, however, sits the founder, owner and sole decision maker - *you*. While some seem to act as though someone else will continually take care of them and clean up the mess, the Young Leader takes full responsibility for all that they say, do and, ultimately, are. Instead of making excuses for their actions, they own them.

They realise they are responsible for their results at work, for what goes in their mouths at every meal, for who is staring back at them in the mirror, for what time they wake in the morning and what time they go to sleep at night. They take responsibility for the thoughts they think, as well as the belief they have in themselves. They realise this life is 100% on them. The good, the bad, the tough, the simple. At the end of the day, the buck stops with them.

Might seem a little harsh. Yet it's the wake-up call many people need. Certainly was for me. I learned that while in some ways I was special and unique, in many other ways, not that many people actually care. No-one is coming to save you.

Every single person that walks this earth has their own life. They've got their own worries, their own struggles, their own baggage and their own history. While some seem to think the universe revolves around them, you and I both know that isn't true. No-one wakes up in the morning with the sole purpose of helping you create the life of your dreams; that's up to you.

These days, people are busy. Really busy. It's not just mail, bills and relaxing on the weekend anymore. It's much, much more. It's 24/7 email responses, work life integration, keeping fit, delighting your customers, managing multiple social networks. All while dealing with emails, texts, snaps, private messages, shout outs and every other form of communication...including communicating in person. And, of course, it's all expected at the drop of a hat. Sorry to sound bleak or cynical, that's just the reality of the world we live in. So is it any wonder that as the responsibilities we now face stack higher and higher, we have increasing tendencies to absolve ourselves from their outcomes?

Unfortunately, a major drawback of the hyper-connected world we live in means we are doing exactly that. Yes, it's brilliant having access to the entire knowledgebase of the world wherever we go, but what many have forgotten to acknowledge is it comes at a cost. That cost is taking responsibility for all that they are. This doesn't just mean taking credit when they do great work (which most don't seem to have a problem with); it includes taking full ownership when things don't go as planned, too. It's about A.P.R. – 'Absolute Personal Responsibility'. No matter what the situation, at any given time the Young Leader will ask themselves "How am I at fault?"

Troubles at home? *How am I at fault?*

Difficult time at work? *How am I at fault?*

Not getting along with someone? *How am I at fault?*

Up until this point, things may have been easy for you or they may have been very hard for you. You may have been dealt a bad hand. Here's the thing though: we've all got a story. We've all had painful times where we weren't sure how we could go on, and we've all had times where everything seemed to feel just right and we wished it could last forever.

From the thousands upon thousands of people I have spent time with over the past few years, there is only one thing each of them has in common: hardship. As Robin Williams states in my favourite movie, Good Will Hunting: "You'll have bad times, but it'll always wake you up to the good stuff you weren't paying attention to."

Either way, what's in the past is in the past, and what I'd like to help you with is realising that all we have is 'now'. Everything that has happened thus far in your life is done. Time to move on.

But how? How can you move on when it seems as though you've been wronged, tricked, let down or cheated on? How does the Young Leader move on despite the perceived baggage they carry with them, while others continually run a story and use that baggage as an excuse for staying small? Two things. Firstly - they release any expectation, and secondly - they own everything they've done in the past, everything they are in the now and everything they will be in the future.

1. Release The Expectation

A few months ago I was struggling with a situation that I wasn't taking full responsibility for. I was upset at the outcome and was blaming others around me for it. At the time, I didn't realise and was playing victim. I spoke with a friend who shared with me a similar experience. He simply said "release the expectation". It was so perfect. No one owes you anything. The stories and outcomes you create in your mind are simply that - stories. When you take full responsibility, you realise you can create what you want, when you want. Release the expectation and set yourself free.

2. Own it

Own the fact that not everything will go your way. Own the fact you've been hurt - because it's made you stronger. Own the fact that you've made mistakes - because they've made you wiser. Own the fact that you've missed opportunities - because they've opened your eyes to new possibilities. And own the fact that you are ready to expand, grow and completely obliterate your old standards from this point forward. The price to pay, if you don't, is a lifetime of blaming others, acting like a victim and allowing the universe to continue sending life's toughest lessons your way until you learn. I don't know about you, but that's not the life I want to live. Have the courage to own your actions today, and let's make sure your future is brighter than your past. Don't be a victim of your past, be the hero of your future.

Learning to take responsibility is difficult. Not only do you have to stay independent from your own story, but you'll also need a lot of faith. Have faith that when you act from your heart, under your best intentions, then eventually the chaos you're experiencing will transform into order. Always remember, life has its own accounting system and it always balances. Stay true to you, and show up every single day as the person you wish to be. You will find your path and, sooner than you think, it will all make sense.

Master Your Habits

Although this book was never intended to have any *how to* sections, there are some essential daily habits of the ultrasuccessful which I wanted to share with you. Modelling the success of the elite is the quickest way to achieve a higher level of success. When you download these success rituals into your human operating system, you can collapse time. If you're able to learn from their mistakes, you can enjoy more of the benefits with less of the downside. There are five success protocols I encourage you to build into your everyday life, which I share with you below.

1. Morning Pages

Three years ago, I purchased a $5 journal from Kmart that ended up becoming a major turning point in my life. It re-shaped how I think, process things and live my life. You might have heard of journaling, or maybe this is your first time. It's the cheapest therapist, the most reliable friend and the best teacher you will ever find. The practice of journaling is one I adhere to most days and something I encourage you to practise also. Around ten months ago, I shared a box of journals with some of my high-end coaching clients who, at the time, were sitting around the table with a confused look on their faces. Many mentioned they didn't know if journaling was for them, or if it would have any benefit. I simply asked them to keep their minds open and get any thoughts that flow into their heads out onto paper. Within weeks they were hooked. Each time I now meet with them, there they are, carrying their little black books.

My journal goes everywhere with me. It's there for any thoughts I have first thing in the morning and also for any thoughts last thing at night. It comes with me to all my meetings and nearly every cafe. Carrying my journal gives me peace of mind. At any point, I know I can scribble ideas, business concepts, new products, marketing campaigns or different plans to take over the world. I draw in it, write lists of priorities and note my frustrations. It's the single most powerful tool I know of to make sense of everything that's going on in my life. It's a current record of how I am feeling and what is happening day to day. It holds my deepest concerns, and also my biggest wins.

As you develop as a Young Leader, your mind will be running at a million miles an hour. Unless you have a system for processing this, your brain will feel like a pinball machine. Ideas will be bouncing around, back and forth, up and down, in and out, without any structure. In the beginning, you might feel as though you can handle it, but as you grow, your mind will continue to take it all in without any way of structuring it. This is where journaling comes in.

Journaling is like magic. It will allow you to get those ideas, thoughts and crazy concepts out of your head and into the world. Some you will pursue while for others, those pages are as far as they'll ever go. But one thing I know for sure is if you don't try, they will forever be stuck in your head taking up precious real estate.

Most shy away from journaling, though. They overthink it and make it complicated. It doesn't have to be hard. Instead, *just write*. There are no rules. Some like to write in list form only; others write letters to themselves. Some write daily, others only when they feel they need to. Some write pages and pages; others write a few lines and are done. I personally write in my journal at least 1 A5 page each morning, inside what I call my 'morning pages'. It sets me up for the day and allows me to process anything I need before the day begins. I channel my 'internal guidance counsellor', who shares with me words of wisdom and advice. The best answers come from within. There are no rules: use whatever system works for you. The only request I have is that you try it. You'll be surprised just how much it can (and will) change the game for you.

2. Get Fit - Stay Fit

It's often surprising when people state they're striving for high performance, peak physical fitness and optimal health, yet their actions tell me otherwise. If you want these things, you'll need to prioritise them. I found personally that the busier I got, the more I neglected my health. What allowed me to achieve high levels of output in the first place was the first to go. When I stopped looking after myself, my energy disappeared, the sharpness of my mind dropped and I became slower. Good leaders lead from the front, and if you're not able to take care of yourself, how are you going to help those you lead?

So many of us take our health for granted. We neglect it until it's needed. Sorry, too late. I remember listening to Robin Sharma recently when he mentioned how a participant at one of his seminars shared a quote: "good health is the crown on the head of a well person that only a sick person can see". Perfect.

Here's a new approach to take: don't just get ready, stay ready. Those who *stay* fit don't need to *get* fit. Health and fitness needs to be built into your lifestyle and become part of your daily non-negotiables (a small list of three-five things you perform every single day, no matter what). Health should be your highest priority. To a person with good health, taking care of themselves is just another item on their list of 1,000 to-do's, but to a person without their health, there is only one to-do: get healthy. Don't let your health slip: work at it.

This might mean going to the gym. It might mean stretching, a yoga class or heading to a boot camp. It might even be going dancing with your partner. Whatever *you* enjoy. Get active, get moving and get fit (really fit), and then stay that way. You won't be sorry.

3. Your Power Hour

If I told you I leap out of bed every morning, I would be doing you a disservice. If I am completely honest, most days I wake up and feel like going back to sleep. However, I don't. I have trained myself to get moving, immediately. I know if I rest my head back on that pillow it is much too easy to fall back into slumberland. If you're anything like me, each morning your mind will try to play tricks on you. No matter how determined we are to change things the night before, when that alarm goes off, our mind is a completely different beast. *Just five more minutes,* it will say. Yet rarely does that five minutes have a positive impact. On the contrary, you nearly always wake up feeling worse.

"But I'm not a morning person!" I hear you say. Sorry to break it to you, but that's a lie. There are no *morning people* or *night people.* Just people. It's a decision - sleep with your dreams, or get up and make them happen. For three or so years now, every day I have been getting up and starting the day before the sun is up. And most days my mind tells me to just sleep for a little longer. Yet I made a decision. No longer did I want to sleep away my life. I'm not saying sleep isn't important - in fact, sleep is absolutely crucial for creativity, energy and longevity, but I knew I can either listen to the tricks of my mind and delay my future, or I can make the choice to get up and continue building my best life.

The way that I developed this skill (and yes, it is a skill - anyone can learn it) is through purpose. The most effective practice I have found for cultivating this purpose is through the creation of a morning routine. A morning routine will give you an incredible sense of accomplishment before most are even awake, while also providing you with the structure necessary to escape from under the covers. While most are warm in their beds, you can be out in the world, making a difference and doing the hard stuff most are too lazy to do.

Right from the get go, you're already ahead. Don't know about you, but I love the feeling of satisfaction first thing in the morning. Like I've got the edge. It keeps me hungry.

Yet how do you structure this morning routine so you actually *want* to get out of bed, rather than sleep for another hour or two? For this, I want to introduce you to something called your 'Power Hour'. This Power Hour (it doesn't have to be an hour, but that's what I recommend to my clients) provides structure to your morning and a reason to get moving. There is only one rule here, and that is you are only allowed to perform activities that fill up *your* cup. Things that replenish *you* and make *you* feel good. As long as the focus is purely on *you*, you're good to go.

Some of the activities you might like to perform first thing are:

- Reading
- Writing your morning pages
- Meditation
- A gratitude practice of some kind
- Stretching
- Exercising
- Watching an educational video
- Listening to an audiobook or podcast

It might sound a little crazy, but all I ask is for you to commit to this practice for thirty days and watch what happens. For the first ten days, you'll probably hate me for suggesting it. The next ten you'll start to see the benefits.

And by day twenty, I'll be your best friend as you continually dominate your day from the moment you wake up.

4. Mind your Inputs

There's an old saying: garbage in, garbage out. It's simple. What you put into your system is what will get out. If you're not careful with what you're feeding the garden of your mind, you'll be forever pulling weeds. You need to be fuelling your mind with positive, uplifting messages on a daily basis. If you're constantly planting news, commercial radio and an array of social media junk, what can you expect to grow in such a garden?

Every time I've felt down or plagued with self-doubt, or known my fears are creeping in (happens to everyone) I fuel my mind with positive inputs. At the loudest volume, I use Youtube clips of Les Brown, Tony Robbins, Robin Sharma, Dr Demartini and other inspirational mentors to flick the switch. I've even recorded my own voice sharing affirmations and positive messages which I'll sometimes listen to in order to spring me back into place.

As humans, we are five times more conditioned to feel negativity and experience doubt than to maximise our potential and dream bigger. The question you need to ask is: am I fuelling my mind with rubbish and forever pulling weeds? Or am I caring for my mind like the wonderful garden of growth it is?

Which reminds me of a concept I learned inside one of my favourite books - *The Magic of Thinking Big* by David

S Schwartz. It's called 'The Thought Factory'. The basic premise is that our minds are a factory, producing various thoughts for us. The quality of these thoughts is determined by what we're fuelling the factory with. If its foreman is 'Mr Triumph', he will constantly be pushing for opportunity, possibility thinking and productivity. If the factory's foreman is 'Mr Defeat', he will be feeding the factory limited thinking, self-doubt and low levels of confidence. In order to stand out as a Young Leader, you need to know which foreman is in charge of your thought factory. Below, I have a few practical activities that you can implement today that will immediately produce results inside your thought factory.

Cut out all TV and News

It's fearmongering at its finest. Take a look at the latest headlines. *'Sick Killer's Insult'*, *'Secret Tapes Bombshell'* and *'You Pay Killer's School Fees'*. Is this the fuel you wish to power your mind with? I haven't read a newspaper or watched the conventional news in five years, and I have not missed a beat. Cut it out and focus on your own goals.

Remove the negative people from your life

People are either in your life for a reason, a season or a lifetime. This isn't good or bad, it just is. Everyone serves a purpose. But what I want you to think about is how you can control the situation. If you fill your environment with junk, what can you expect to get in return? It might sound strange, but a little while ago, I created a 'friends' list. Jim

Rohn famously stated "you are the average of the five people you spend the most time with". So, I made the decision I only wanted to spend time with those who inspired me and wrote out the names of the five people I wanted as friends. Over the coming months that is exactly what happened, and today I am fortunate enough to be surrounded by big thinkers. Make your friends list and watch the magic of the universe unfold.

<u>Environment dictates performance</u>

A good mentor of mine is Australia's best high-performance real estate coach, Josh Phegan. When figuring out what a person is like, he uses the 'three environments test'. Josh asks a series of questions based around three key environments: their car, their home and their office. Below, I paraphrase Josh's big idea.

If we jumped in your car right now, would there be empty takeaway wrappers, old clothes and a bunch of junk on the seats? Or would it be clean, smell fresh and have everything sorted? If we went to your house, would the floor be lined with clothes, items randomly placed everywhere and look like a bomb hit it? Or are things structured? A place for everything and everything in its place? Lastly, if we went to your office, does it look like somewhere that a million-dollar earner sits? Or is it filled with messy papers, documents and rubbish?

People often underestimate just how much impact your environment can have on your outcomes. Clean up your three environments and watch what it does to your mental clarity.

5. Become an Artist and Master your Craft

I consider myself an artist. Instead of paint, I use words. Instead of a brush, I use a keyboard. I love stringing words together like a painter places strokes upon his easel. The words flow from my fingers as if possessed. I crave writing. I wake up and think about it. I go to sleep and think about it.

You too are an artist. Art is whatever you want it to be. A creative release. A way to express yourself. All we need to do is find it. Once we do, it's game over. Nothing is more powerful than a Young Leader with a master plan ahead of them. When the Young Leader applies themselves to their art, magic happens. They take on the challenge, embrace the difficulties and continually strive to become better. Discover your art, find your easel and then commit yourself to mastery.

Implementing (and sticking to) new habits

Here's the thing – while motivation is high and you're in a productive state of mind from reading the above, it's easy to fall into the illusion that growing these habits will simply happen. Just stick to it for 66 days and it will become permanent, right? Or is it 21 days? What's the latest research again?

Many quasi scientists seem to blindly quote the number of days it takes to implement a new habit based on something they read years or even decades ago, using a skewed sample and inconclusive results. Don't know about you, but I'd prefer to have something a little more reliable than that, which is what I want to share with you next.

Basic human behaviour dictates that you will only ever act when you see more positive than negative. This means that the greatest indicator of whether or not you will adopt a new habit is directly based upon how you see that specific activity benefiting what's most important to you. The clearer you see it, the greater the likelihood you'll stick to it.

Feeling Cloudy?

What if you can't see it, though? Or maybe you've tried but are having trouble maintaining the habit? Does it mean you have no willpower? Are destined to keep failing? Nope. This is where the magic come in. All you need to do is help your brain see some of the benefits. This is done through an exercise called '*stacking*'. All you need to do is list 50, 100 or 200+ benefits of adopting the habit until you see clearly, without hesitation, how this habit will help you towards what's most important to you and serve you in your life. The more links you create, the higher the probability you will stick to the habit. Conversely, if there is a habit you wish to stop, simply stack the drawbacks of that habit and how it's actually negatively affecting that which is most important to you.

Healthy habits create a healthy life.

Be Like Nike.

So many I see, though, have trouble getting started. They tell me every story under the sun why they can't do it: *it's not for me, I don't really want it, it's not that important to me.* Unless they're paying me, I usually just smile and nod. Sometimes, though, if I can see it's actually important to them, I'll ask: "Have you heard of Nike?" A little confused, they usually reply: "Ah, yeah?", "Well, *just do it,*" I reply. They look back at me, shocked. It sounds too easy. Yet if your goal is to increase your impact and influence, at some point you're going to need to make a choice to throw yourself in and just. do. it.

Too many on this earth delay their futures, attempting to make everything more complicated than it needs to be. They're the first to hesitate, procrastinate and complain, but the last to actually put in the required work to be where they want to be. Time to take control. Stop pressing snooze on your dreams. Instead, make a choice. It's either *From this point I'm going to step up and take full control* or *From this point I'm going to continue playing small, doing things by half, and just continue to get by.* Your call.

The perfect time is now

I get it, though. At some point, we've all seen someone else's success and been guilty of thinking "Man, that should've been me...I would've done it way better". Well, let me ask, why didn't you? You keep telling yourself it should be you, yet you're waiting for the right time, the right opportunity, the right people, the right place and the right everything before you make a move.

Let me help you. There is no right place. There is no right time. There is no right opportunity. There are no right people. There is only one way to see if something is 'right', and that is by actually doing it. Sometimes it works out; other times you need to change direction and try again. But if you don't try, you don't know, and if you don't know, you'll die wondering.

Let's face it, you're never going to be ready. Guess what? Do it anyway.

Things aren't perfect? Do it anyway.

Timing isn't right? Do it anyway.

Not smart enough? Do it anyway.

Don't have the experience? Do it anyway.

The story you're telling yourself about things needing to be perfect before you start, is simply that...a story. Truth is, 99.9999% of people won't even care. And if they do care about you having a go, getting yourself out there and forging a new path, they're simply reflecting feelings of insecurity and jealousy from within. Most likely, they're wishing they had the same courage you've applied in putting yourself out there, and their comments are representative of that.

But this isn't just about you anymore. It goes far beyond that. Despite what you might've been told by the dream-takers along your journey, our world needs you. I believe within each of us, there is a unique gift. A precious elixir unique to our being. By hiding this inner gold within and allowing your fears to win, you're doing the world a disservice. No-one was put on this earth to play small, and by listening to the opinions of others, you're not having the impact we need. Hundreds, thousands and even millions of people are going without because for too long they have been listening to the doubters and trying to please everyone but themselves.

There is only one thing on this earth that has the true answers, and that is your heart. Your heart never fails you. It is there when you wake up and there when you go to sleep. Until the minute it stops beating, its sole purpose is to keep you alive and guide you on your path.

Yet most won't listen to this internal guidance system. Instead, they wait for a sign or a saviour. Anything other than doing the work. Well, guess what? The wait is over. Imagine if Richard Branson had waited. We would all be paying through the roof for airfares. Imagine if Steve Jobs had waited. We would all still have computers with line commands and black and white screens. Imagine if Henry Ford had waited. We would all still be getting around in a horse and cart (maybe).

We all have our vices, and if you feel like you're 'not ready', welcome to the club. No-one ever feels ready. Yet every single person on this earth that has had an impact in any way, shape or form has at some point made that decision to be like Nike and Just. Do. It.

Next time you're faced with a decision, don't think it over. Don't plan for weeks, don't poll everyone around you and don't put it off. Simply listen from within your heart and do what you feel is right. Less wishing, more working. Less dreaming, more doing. Don't sit by as a passive follower and rely on others to call the shots in your life. Become the master of your destiny and create your best life. Isn't it about time?

Embracing Confusion

So far, we have discussed what it's like to show up with the right attitude, willing and ready to make a difference. But what if you're in a funk? What if you have read the above but have no idea how you're going to make it happen?

It's one thing to show up when things are going well, but an entirely different thing to do so when things aren't going so well. We all go through tough times, and we all have times of self-doubt. While most struggle to get moving and take the desired action toward their goals, leaders have the ability to use the unwelcome feelings of confusion and uncertainty as fuel.

My goal here is to help switch your thinking to understand that, despite how it might seem, the difficulties you may face and the challenges you may encounter along your journey are all part of a hidden order that exists within the universe. When you discover this hidden order, you will not see situations as 'good' or 'bad', but, instead, you will see them for what they really are - outcomes.

All experiences, both negative and positive, have in some way, shape or form provided you with the tools necessary to continually grow and expand your current reality. Each has provided a particular skill designed to help you gain the necessary strength to continue. Yet many don't see this. They continue to play victim and fail to see what is in plain sight to the rest of us. Everything you have done (or not done) up until this point has been guiding you perfectly along your journey to create your own personal legend.

As humans, at times we are prone to experiencing feelings of being lost or without direction (what some may label 'depression'). However, bouts of this so-called 'depression' are completely normal. In fact, I argue they are necessary.

While no human desires the feeling of confusion, the Young Leader understands that all confusion is followed by clarity. Instead of shying away from confusion, they embrace it. Inside the chaos, they strive to master their emotions and remove the variability of 'ups and downs', taking solace in the fact that one day (sooner than you think) things will once again return to *normal*. Just like they always have.

All life is a constant mix of support and challenge. Good and bad. Easy and hard. Instead of asking "why me?", switch the questioning - "what is life trying to teach me?" - because with great challenge comes great growth.

Drop the label

But it won't just happen. Growth will only occur when we stand up and take responsibility. When you place labels upon yourself (or are given said labels via a doctor or 'specialist'), your behaviour will adapt as such. One of the most prevalent labels in society right now is 'depression'.

I don't believe people should associate themselves with *having* depression. This is dangerous. By giving yourself the title of *having* depression, you are providing yourself with justification for the 'condition'. Using such labels is counterproductive to removing unwanted feelings of isolation and loneliness that accompany such a state. When you attach this label, you begin to associate and behave as someone with such a label, thus fuelling the perpetuating cycle of self-hate and hopelessness. No matter what, we will only ever do something that provides more benefit than drawback. Despite what many like to think (or admit), this is a reality of human behaviour.

While I do recognise that, yes, the science may tell you people who suffer from what today is most commonly labelled 'depression' will have significantly reduced levels of the neurotransmitters Serotonin and Norepinephrine, 'depression' itself is a natural part of life, helping you realise you're off track. Please understand that this is not medical advice and that each and every situation is different. If you wish to pursue a different path, you're more than welcome. I am simply sharing my opinion and offering you an alternative method to dealing with feelings of depression, anxiety and, possibly, extreme sadness than what most conventional doctors seemingly suggest. Unfortunately, many profit-driven pharmaceutical companies, and yes, they are companies who make billions upon billions of dollars each year, are courting doctors to essentially bribe them into increased prescriptions of what we can call 'band-aid' fix medication. These so-called medications, which have risen in supply and administration dramatically over the past decade, prove that, rather than working through the issues, we are constantly looking for a quick fix. What's of even greater concern is that these medications are now also being prescribed to children. Add to that the fact that many studies provide evidence on placebo medications having the exact same positive benefits as these overprescribed medications, and that the general 'benefits' don't kick in for at least six to twelve weeks, and something needs to be done.

What many don't realise (or prefer to remain oblivious to) is the harsh side effects that accompany these pills and the fact that by ingesting these tablets, you aren't really addressing the underlying issues. Instead, you're opting to numb and avoid what is really happening. While some may argue such medications are a good starting point and can kickstart your emotions back to 'normal', I don't agree. There are other, more effective, options, especially in the long term, which we explore below.

The Seasons of Life

I believe that in life, sometimes we are happy, other times we are sad. Sometimes we are clouded with confusion, other times we act with absolute certainty. If it were always one way or the other, we would never grow. It's during these states of so-called 'depression' that we derive our greatest power or purpose for the future. Order arises not in spite of the confusion, but because of it. These feelings of increased chaos will continue until a single decision point is arrived at. We can call this the 'Breaking Point'. From here, two paths are revealed - one leading to 'Breakdown', the other leading to 'Breakthrough'.

Would it be true to say during your life you've had moments where it all seemed too much? Like you couldn't go on? Yet isn't it also true that if you're reading this, you did manage to go on? While many believe during these times they are alone, I want to assure you it's all a part of what we can call 'the seasons of life'. This is a completely normal experience and one we all go through at some point. The longer it lasts, the longer you are neglecting the signs the universe is attempting to share with you on how to get back on track.

Yet complications begin when we once again attach unnecessary labels. I have seen some of the best mindset practitioners shift years of negative self-talk and self-hatred to help their clients come out the other side within a few weeks, days and, in some cases, hours with a completely transformed outlook on life. No prescription drugs, no manipulation, just the right line of questioning to invoke the inner inspiration waiting within. With the right questions, not only is this possible, but highly probable. You are not alone in this battle. Do not attempt to hide from the confusion. Embrace it. It means you are one step closer to a newer, even greater reality. Remember, the tighter an arrow is drawn back upon the bow, the further it will fly.

The Journey

While a good leader understands that at times, self-talk will be part of the journey, they also understand it shouldn't *be* the journey. You were not put on this earth to continually struggle, fight and demoralise yourself. In fact, quite the opposite. You were put on this earth to achieve greatness. To move our society forward in your own unique way. Now get out of your own head and out into the world to make a difference.

To help aid in the 'recovery' process I wanted to share two approaches with you: 'reflection' and 'progression'.

Reflection

To create change within the mind, we need to take the time to reflect objectively. When we feel depressed or anxious, it's because we've created an unrealistic expectation of what life should be, rather than what it is. The greater the gap, the more unfulfilled we feel. This only worsens as we fixate and obsess over the lives of others, while of course only looking at the good stuff and ignoring the bad stuff. As a consequence, we develop extremely low self-esteem and self-image.

To alleviate this, you must acknowledge your strengths and begin to appreciate the self again. One helpful method of doing this is to use what I call the 'What I Know' list. I created it when I was feeling particularly down, negative and confused, and it really helped. During such times negativity fills the mind and seeking 'safety' (instead of addressing the real issue), we start chasing the quick fix. This only leads to furthering our fantasies and false hopes, while we ride the emotional rollercoaster. The promise of a greater future and quick fix sounds exciting to begin with, but when the reality kicks in that the universe is always in perfect balance, you realise that no matter what the situation, there is always a price to pay.

The single best way to combat the doubt and uncertainty plaguing your mind is through the 'What I Know' list. All you need is a blank journal and around ten minutes. On a new page, simply write at the top: "I know I...." followed by writing something you know (*in your heart of hearts*) to be true. That is, if anyone were to argue with you, you could (and would) argue to the death. It's something that deep down you know with absolute certainty, and nothing could change your mind.

Continue the process by again writing: "I know I..." on the next line. Repeat for as long as needed. With each line, you will be creating more and more certainty within. For example, I know I am a good writer. I know I host great events. I know I love interviewing world leaders and interesting people. Start with what you know and let what you know, grow. So, what do you know?

<u>Progression</u>

The second key to getting things back on track is to get moving. I've learned that when we feel 'depressed', it can often be boiled down to the fact we're not progressing. Life is one long journey of ever-increasing knowledge and growth. If we're not growing, we're dying. Each time I see someone with the symptoms of so-called depression, they always have one thing in common - stagnation. They're stuck in the same job without progression. They're not learning anything new. They're following someone else's personal legend as opposed to their own. So is it any wonder they don't feel good?

I compare this to a stagnant lake. Not only is the lake a breeding ground for bacteria, but also a cesspool bathing in its own filth. It doesn't move and constantly remains the same. This is exactly how some choose to live their lives. If we choose to stay stagnant, we become the lake.

Now let's compare that with a river. A river flows freely, with fresh water passed down from a higher power. It crafts its own path and does not stop. Instead, it is forever evolving and expanding over the bank as it grows. While the lake simply sits around, waiting for something to happen, the river is constantly working as far as it can reach to provide fresh water for the trees and nature surrounding it.

When we choose to get things moving again, like the river, we experience feelings of flow and forward momentum. Flowing like the river allows you to find the real you. The one who knows what you love, what makes you happy, what activities you enjoy and how you like to feel. Which begs the question: where can we find this real you?

Get Moving

One of the simplest ways to do so is through exercise. A run, a ride, a gym session, a walk, a yoga class or running up the stairs thirty times. It's immediate and tangible, and can be performed anywhere, anytime. Instead of waiting six to twelve weeks for 'medication' to kick in, we can see benefits almost immediately, *without any side effects*. Lifts go up, running times get quicker, the body starts feeling better with the release of positive emotions. I'm not talking about setting world records in the gym, nor running a marathon (although that could be a good long-term goal to give you something to work towards), but, instead, just getting you moving. Maybe all you need is to start with the goal of moving for five minutes every single day for the next thirty days? Maybe you could sign up to work with a personal trainer one day a week? Maybe you could start with 10 push-ups a day for the next week, before moving onto 11 next week, then 12?

Apart from the proven benefits of raised endorphins - life's natural happiness drug - we are getting you moving again. Both physically and metaphorically. You are no longer stagnant like the lake, but, instead, flowing like the river. Get up, get moving, get active. Let your heart rate rise and sweat drip from your brow. All life is progress and the sooner you realise, the sooner you can get things back on track.

Anyone can show up, but it takes real effort to show up at 100%, ready to take action on your goals and shift your reality day in, day out. Yet this is how *real* change is created. The more you avoid so-called 'problems', the more they will continually appear in your life. Don't use labels to hide; instead, use the above to discover how your confusion is serving you and what the universe is attempting to help you realise. Stop avoiding, start listening. Stop complaining, start living. Stop putting it off, get started today and let's get you (re)inspired.

Let Rejection Fuel You

What happens, though, when you try your hardest, you put in the work and you take the risks, yet things *still* don't work out as you had planned? Failure and rejection often halt our progress and can make us feel as if our efforts up until this point have been wasted. When we experience rejection, we have two options. Either take the hit and accept defeat, or continue to show up, learn the lesson and ride on. From the outside, leadership may seem glamorous, yet a major part of the journey is accepting the certain rejection you'll face along the way. The job you wanted fell through, the guy or girl you asked out doesn't get back to you, the client goes with a competitor. It's virtually impossible not to be immediately affected emotionally when these things happen. There are going to be plenty of disappointments along your journey, and while it's okay to grieve, at some point you need to accept the fact it's happened and move on. The time it takes to discover the lesson is what we call wisdom. The sooner you can find the once hidden lesson, the wiser you are.

Saying this, however, is one thing; acting upon it is another. In this chapter, I share a unique approach to dealing with the certain rejection you'll inevitably face along your journey.

Of the exceptional leaders I have been lucky enough to learn from, not one has a story free of heartache and tribulation. Some grew up poor and had to fight their way to the top; others were born into money but had to fight against the stereotype that money somehow does the hard work for you. Some had vicious rumours spread about them; others had upbringings that would bring you to your knees. Yet they fought through. Instead of playing victim to their circumstances, they worked at what worked. In life, you get what you focus on. Focus on the junk, you will get junk. Focus on the good stuff, you will get more good stuff. Rejection doesn't get any easier, but the way you manage it does. It's this process that will determine whether you continue to wallow in a pool of self-pity, or you suit up, ready for battle because you know you can handle it.

No-one *started* successful

The interesting thing about success, though, is that no-one started that way. No-one started with a multimillion-dollar business. No-one started as the most influential person in their industry. No-one started as the CEO or chairman of a company, and no-one started off with every skill required to be an effective leader. Richard Branson started the Virgin empire with the same 168 hours in a week both you and I have. Arnold Schwarzenegger has the same number of muscles in his body as we all have. Mark Zuckerberg started Facebook and changed the way the world communicates using the same books, resources and computer systems we all have access to (remember, once upon a time he was just a college student with no networks and barely any money).

So why is it that these people have been able to achieve things that were once seen as impossible, while others cannot even seem to get moving? You can blame genetics, poor upbringing, lack of funding and a plethora of other external factors, but the truth is, these people weren't overly fortunate in their circumstances. Even if you do argue that luck played a part, understand that luck might be the .01% to get you in the door, but if you want to stay there, the other 99.99% is a refined skillset that has been built from years of taking rejection on the chin and moving forward regardless of the setbacks encountered.

Success Scars

Thing is, every successful leader has a list of tough learned lessons they've experienced along their journey. It's part of the deal. These success scars act as a reminder for the battles they've overcome. Instead of giving up in the face of adversity, successful leaders have the ability to focus on the opportunity within a situation, rather than the drawbacks. An unrelenting desire to create a new way of doing things, rather than accepting the norm, along with the tenacity to reject mediocrity and craft a new path forward is what defines their success.

Take Elon Musk, for example. One man, with the same number of eyes, limbs and ears and the same physical structure as most of us. Yet this same man has been able to revolutionise space travel, solar power, electric cars and a variety of other industries too. Is he different? Does he really have anything you don't (or can't) have? Not by a long shot. He was just prepared to create the reality he wanted to live. The late Steve Jobs, co-founder of Apple stated once that "life can be much broader once you discover one simple fact: Everything around you that you call life was made up by people that were no smarter than you and you can change it, you can influence it, you can build your own things that other people can use." Love it.

If you're willing to go through the same pain and challenges as those you perceive as more successful than you, then you too can receive such rewards.

What you don't see

The shift I want to help you see is that while on the surface things may look seamless, behind every successful idea are a thousand terrible ones. Behind every successful business are ten failed ideas. Behind every overnight success, there are countless hours of behind the scenes work that no-one will ever know about. Proposals that got rejected. Deals that were supposed to happen, but never went through. People saying one thing, but doing another. Dishonest employees or friends, plus thousands of hours spent inside books, seminars and conversations.

What most don't really like to look at (as it would burst their bubble and open their eyes to the fact they themselves aren't doing the actual work required for such an impact) is that day after day, week after week, year after year and decade after decade, successful individuals have continually been working at their dreams. Through hardship and challenge, they found what worked and did more of that, while painfully finding out what didn't work, and doing less of that. Sometimes it was easy and sometimes it was hard. The armchair commentators and 'haters' will simply observe those achieving success while never fully understanding that things weren't always that way. Unaware of the price that was paid and the sacrifices that were made along the journey. They fail to see the scars that with time may have healed, but will never be forgotten. Guess that's why they're stuck commentating, while others are succeeding.

Young Leaders stick to their own paths, stay in their own lane and run their own race. In a world full of talkers, focus on you and yours. It's the only way to continue toward your own journey of greatness. Decide right here, right now, which side of the fence you will fall on and then go all in.

I promise it will be worth it...

PART 2: STAND OUT

"Luck is what happens when preparation meets opportunity."
- Seneca the Great

If Woody Allen was right, and 80% of success is showing up, standing out must be the other 20%. You can be in the right place at the right time, but if you aren't prepared, you will miss your shot.

You need to make sure that when your opportunity comes around, you're there with arms wide open, ready to grab what's already yours.

The truth is, opportunity is all around us. Sometimes it's in plain sight; other times, it's wrapped inside a package for us that looks a lot like heartache, pain or confusion. When you learn how to discover the hidden opportunity within and start to see every opportunity for what it is (growth) you begin to embrace life with a completely new outlook.

Part two of this book will prepare you for that. We start by looking at how you approach learning, before introducing you to the four stages of an idea and how to deal with so-called 'failure'. I then share with you a simple method you can use to reach anyone on the planet while getting what you want, called the 'power of ask'. I finish off by helping you discover a thought process that will challenge your thinking.

Don't just stand up, stand out. Let's grow.

Always be a Student of the Game

You can be at the right place at the right time, but if you've got the wrong attitude, you'll be running in circles. Standing out as a Young Leader is all about developing and maintaining an open mind when it comes to learning. As a Young Leader (and human being), how much you learn dictates how much you earn. Learning arms you with the appropriate weapons to fight for your cause. Learning is the lifeblood of any Young Leader. In this chapter, we explore the approach I encourage you to take if you want to stand out and soak up the lessons life throws at you.

Around six months ago, I was watching a presentation hosted by one of my mentors, Dr John Demartini. Dr Demartini speaks full time around the world (300-400 engagements per year), has coached some of the most successful people in the world, including presidents of major countries, gold medal winning Olympic athletes and CEO's of billion-dollar organisations, while also being considered by many to be at the top of his field (human behaviour and maximising human potential).

During the presentation, someone asked Dr Demartini what it was that continues to drive his hunger for success and constant improvement after being in this field for over 44 years. Dr Demartini paused for a moment and humbly stated "well...I always just consider myself *under construction.*" Brilliant. *Under construction.* Two words that will forever be tattooed on my brain. If someone with nearly four and a half decades of experience in one field still considers themselves *under construction,* you cannot help but be inspired to continue your own journey of excellence.

To achieve the highest level of success in your field, you will always need to remain a student of the game. To enter each and every situation with a white belt mentality. Like a true beginner, your ego needs to be left at the door to allow your mind to stay open to new possibilities. This mentality will allow you to tackle problems with all the enthusiasm and passion of a beginner learning something for the first time. Young Leaders embrace each opportunity with a deep hunger for growth and a passion to become more than they currently are, while also having the drive to take action.

Become a Lifer

It's from here that you will be able to develop what I call a 'lifer' mentality. Traditionally a term used to describe a prison inmate with a life sentence, a 'lifer' is anyone who is dedicated to something they love, *for life.* A lifer lets nothing get in the way. A lifer doesn't create excuses, they create solutions. I am a lifer for the gym. Back in 2010, I broke my foot while training on the football field two days out from my first game. I was put into a plastic moon boot that went halfway up my leg and forced me to use crutches to prevent my putting any weight onto my left leg for eight weeks. At the time, I was heavily into the gym, so people kept asking me what I would do without it. I didn't understand what they meant. Why would it be an issue? I was in a boot and on crutches, not a quadriplegic. As far as I saw it, I had perfectly good use of over three quarters of my body. So, I continued using the gym and doing what I could.

That's what a lifer does. For a lifer, it is never a question of *if*, but *how*. In the face of adversity, instead of giving up and conceding defeat, a lifer just does what they do best - they continue.

The Man in Blue

Late last year, at around 6.30 pm on Christmas Eve, I was sitting by an oval, reflecting and taking stock of how the year had been inside my journal. Out the corner of my eye, I saw a blue speck moving. I shifted my eyes to see a man in a blue shirt running laps around the oval. "Pretty cool," I thought. I always get inspired by those putting in work.

As he makes his way over my side of the oval, I see he is around 55 years old. Looks ultra-fit though. You can just tell those legs have some k's in them. Here we are, early evening the night before Christmas and this guy is just doing his thing. No audience, no accolades, no selfies, just a man quietly running his own race. He runs past me six times, seven times, eight times. He could easily stop, who would even notice? Yet he doesn't. In fact, he takes things a step further. On the opposite side of the oval he drops down and does 20 or so push-ups before jumping back to his feet and resuming his laps. Another lap, another 20 push-ups. In the end, I'd say he did 14 or 15 laps. I lost count but it was truly inspiring. The thing is, if I had gone over and spoken with him (which I wanted to, but didn't want to interrupt his rhythm) I don't believe he would see it as noble or anything out of the ordinary. He was just doing what he loves. The perfect embodiment of what it means to be a lifer. A true legend of the game.

Here's the big idea though: for a lifer, none of this seems abnormal. It isn't tough, it isn't difficult and it isn't unusual. The lifer just simply does what they love to do.

Learning[3]

So often, though, people don't take advantage of the lessons and teachers surrounding them. They think the only way to learn is from people 'above' them. When you think this way, you miss out on the valuable lessons right in front of you. While the experience of others is vitally important, it's not the whole story. To stand out you need to surround yourself with the following three types of people: those above you, those at the same level as you and those below you. Let's explore.

Those above you

These are the people who can mentor you, coach you, guide you, share wisdom with you and see you succeed (and, of course, see you fail). They've done more than you, they've felt the pain of failure and they want to help you progress without feeling the same pain.

Those at the same level

These are people who will help support you, but also challenge you. They will constantly be growing, just like you, and this healthy push is essential in your growth. In some ways, you inspire them through the action you take and in other ways, they inspire you with the action they take. You both use this as fuel and feed off each other.

Those below you

These are people whom you are teaching, mentoring and offering advice to. The brilliance of this group is that we grow best when we teach others, meaning that even though this group is below us, often this is where we stand to learn the most. This group keeps your mind sharp - pushing you to fully understand concepts and think of alternative ways to succeed.

To be an exceptional Young Leader, you need to maintain a balance of these three people in your life. Doing so will keep you in sync. If things don't feel right, it's usually because one of these three aren't in place.

We were put on this earth to learn, share and grow. All of us are here to pass the torch. Have a think about who you're learning *from*, who you're growing *with* and who you're helping *inspire* and *push* to new levels. If you don't know, find them. It will help you develop as a leader.

Serving Your Apprenticeship

There is one step, however, that you do not want to miss in your learning journey. It's called 'serving your apprenticeship'. Every single one of us who wants to have an impact on the world (using our own business as a catalyst), should first work for someone else.

This is where you will learn the valuable and useful skills that are necessary to obtain (and maintain) a client within the marketplace. Without these skills, you will constantly struggle. From my personal experience, and studying some of the best leaders, the best place to get them is inside a small business with a growth-minded founder. There are six key reasons I say this.

1. Small businesses generally don't have large budgets. This means you will learn how to become resourceful and frugal with money.

2. You'll get close and have direct access to the founder/their close network. Their lessons will be valuable for you. Soak them up like a sponge. At every opportunity ask to be involved, go the extra mile, put yourself in situations that force you to grow and be around as much as you can.

3. You'll have to wear multiple different hats. Your skill set will expand almost daily. This is a blessing. Take on new challenges and run with them.

4. You'll be directly accountable for results. Results are the lifeblood of any business. You can't hide in a two-six person team for very long.

5. These businesses generally have a model that works – ie, it's making sales. It might need tweaking (or significant overhaul), but if they have at least a

second person working, things must be going okay for now. This means they know what is valuable in the marketplace. Learn why it is valuable and seek as much feedback on that as possible. It will be very useful when designing your own product or service down the track.

6. You won't get lost in the machine. Inside a large corporate, you can get away with flying under the radar for far too long (I went for two years back in 2010 because there was very little accountability - they didn't even notice). It not only eats your soul, but you soon get sick of browsing the internet all day, aimlessly. Humans need purpose.

I was genuinely fortunate to serve my apprenticeship with two people who helped me grow significantly. Personally and professionally. This included what to do, but also what not to do. The good stuff showed me how to run things and provided experience in each of the above, while the bad stuff drove me to improve so I would never be in that situation again. I am grateful for both.

While many will bark that you need to work for yourself, instead of making someone else 'rich', I highly encourage every young person to first serve their apprenticeship under someone else before heading out on their own.

The balancing act here is not to leave too early, but also not to get trapped there. You're the only one who can make that call. Choose wisely.

Make More Mistakes

But even when you've had the best mentors, read a library worth of books and attended a long list of seminars, there is one teacher who shares with us our greatest lessons. She is a strict taskmaster and an even stricter disciplinarian. She is quick to reprimand and slow to reward. She can be very cruel or very kind. But if you follow her rules, you will reap her rewards. This is what we call 'life.'

But what are those rules? At this point, maybe you'd expect some simple 'how to' instructions, right? Get up earlier, eat a healthy diet, exercise regularly, etc. All *that* stuff. Let me ask you though...if 'how to' worked, why aren't we all six percent body fat with washboard abs and a Ferrari parked in the garage? In reality, we do not need more 'how to'. Despite what the gurus attempt to sell you, 'how to' is *not* the magic key you've been searching for. 'How to' is broken, a lie you've been sold for too long.

With the overwhelming amount of information we have access to growing every day, we are constantly bombarded with 'secrets', 'insights', 'top ten lists' and 'bullet-proof blueprints' for 'success'. Yet when you look carefully, the rewards you seek are not found within some elusive pot of gold at the end of the rainbow. Instead, they're wrapped inside the lessons we learn along the way. The gold is always found in the journey, not the destination.

My goal for you within these pages (and your life) is not to provide you with more 'how to', but, instead, with the right questions to ask yourself in order to craft your own path. To write your own story. A reality *you* can create based on what *you* want and the things that personally inspire *you* - not what some four-step success system promises you. This is what drives me, and what I see as the path forward for those looking to master their lives. Once you know what questions to ask, no longer are you trapped by some guru up on the mountaintop, or reliant on him sharing with you his supposed infinite wisdom. Instead, you become your own guru.

Constant Comparison

Which begs the question: why are we so desperately looking for 'how to'? What magic do we think it will provide? My guess? Fear. In today's ultra-connected world, where there are no secrets, not only do we fear looking like a failure amongst our friends, peers and, ironically, a bunch of cyber strangers, but beyond that, our greatest fear is of not being enough. Not smart enough, not rich enough, not successful enough, not good looking enough. No matter what we do, we feel as though it's never enough. With one swipe of our finger on our smartphones we now gain a direct insight into the previously private lives of those all around us. We scroll the highlight reel of their lives and think; why isn't *my* life like that? Why aren't *I* climbing mountains, buying flashy new cars or getting engaged? Why am *I* so far behind? We unfairly compare our chapter 1 to someone else's chapter 20. It's this unrealistic fantasy that is impossible to reach that causes us pain.

It's all perception-based. From this place of scarcity, we search for some imaginary magic bullet designed to shortcut us to success. To get the pleasure without the pain. The support without the challenge. The wins without the losses. Yet who is brave enough to admit that it doesn't exist? When was the last time you were able to bypass the bad and shoot straight to the good? And was it truly worth it? Or, if you're completely honest with yourself, did it feel empty? The reason 97% of lottery winners go broke within the first 12 months of winning is that they're not ready for such rewards. Those who receive without paying the price quickly find those rewards will be lost.

In order to create, sustain and grow the rewards you seek, a price must be paid. Upfront and in full. In life, that price is becoming a person who is ready to receive said rewards. In all cases, this requires you to rise to the challenge and face the demands of success. To bare all and, at times, risk everything you've worked for. The greatest teacher you'll ever find is not the books you read or the mentors you work with, but the mistakes you make along the way. For it's these mistakes in which we experience our greatest growth.

The thing is, while the masses are looking for less challenge, less discomfort and less difficulty, the masters recognise all life is challenge. Instead of shying away from challenge, they simply choose challenges that inspire them. That way, all experiences (both good and bad) become part of the journey. The lessons learned along the way are seen as another speed bump, not a great chasm that can't be crossed.

Don't be afraid of these challenges, embrace them. Through the pain and suffering, you will come out the other side with more strength than you ever thought possible.

Who are you growing into?

As seekers who constantly strive for growth, every single day we are wanting more. This internal desire to be more than we were yesterday fuels our hunger for growth. The complication to this approach is that rarely do we feel as though things are 'finished'. Take this book for example. Each day I would go to submit it to my editor, yet each day I would develop new ideas to continually input. What you're reading is an accumulation of my deepest thoughts and learnings from my life. It includes every piece of wisdom I've learned from my mentors, books, courses, conversations, jobs and, of course, mistakes, throughout my 29 trips around the sun.

Thing is, as a seeker, it's easy to get caught in the curse of perfection. Every day I see new lessons, learnings, ways of interpreting things and growth opportunities. With my highest value being my writing, I love being able to share those lessons with others through my words. Yet if it wasn't for a mentor sharing his advice, the very words you read would still be bouncing around inside my head. Waiting and waiting until the perfect time to launch. My mentor's advice was to just get it out there: "a book is simply a representation of our thoughts, beliefs, theories and unique point of view at any one point in time." He was right. I could sit here, procrastinating, adding, removing and tweaking forever. However, once I shifted my thinking to see my book as a 'thought time capsule' to share with the world, I became free. What started off as a small 20-page guide designed to introduce me to publishing something quickly turned into 50 pages, which then turned into what you hold within your hands. Yes, I could have kept writing. My love of writing and curiosity for life's lessons could see a book quickly expand to 100,000+ words if I wasn't careful. Instead, I decided to focus my energy on producing the very best record of my current thinking. I came to peace with the fact that this will change. My mind will grow and my thoughts will expand. I let go of seeing this as a burden and opened up to seeing it as an opportunity. An opportunity to evolve, extend and continually become a stronger version of myself. Is there anything you're putting off? Anything being plagued by the curse of perfection? Stop it. Literally, it's that easy. Stop putting it off, seal up the time capsule and ship it to the world. It's time.

Student to Teacher

But what next? As humans, we love learning, but to learn without teaching is not really learning at all. A major part of the learning process is passing the torch to others and sharing what we learn. However, there is this strange thing that happens when we learn something new, that nearly all of us fall victim to. Let me share what I mean through my own experience:

When I first discovered lifting weights. I became obsessed (and I mean obsessed). My conversations would revolve around it. I'd wake up and think about it. I'd talk about it to anyone who would listen. Even if they wouldn't listen, I'd still talk about it. Reps, sets, programmes, exercises, protein, carbs, fats, good fats, trans fats, monounsaturated fats, rest days, biceps, triceps, quadriceps and everything in between. I could literally speak for hours on my new-found passion. Problem was, the audience (friends and family) didn't understand a word I was saying. It was like a foreign tongue. Pretty soon I would sense (or see) their eyes roll over when I got going and recognised they probably didn't care as much as I did.

Looking back now, I can see what I was doing was a classic beginner mistake. When we're passionate about something high on our values system, we get excited. Really excited. We want to share it with the world, so we do. We tell everyone we know. Just like with my weight lifting, however, not everyone is as passionate about the topic as us. It's not that people don't care (although most won't), it's just they don't really understand. The key here is not to turn your passion off or try to hide it, but, instead, share it with those who are equally passionate. Find your tribe. And if you can't find one, create one. There are so many passionate people in this world and with the internet it is now easier than ever to find other wacky, weird, unusual humans just like you and me. Open your eyes, open your heart and discover those who are on this journey with you.

Meet them downstream

Of course there will be times when you need to teach someone who might not see the reason for learning a certain lesson, but you know it will be critical for their growth. In these situations, instead of expecting others to change and adapt to your style, you may have to shift your teaching style to help them see how the information you're sharing will help them achieve that which is most important to them.

I have a particular friend who would constantly come to me having issues inside his business. None of his staff seemed to 'get it'. He would tell me how he's showed them time and time again, repeatedly told them what to do, yet for some reason it just wasn't getting through. Each time he'd describe what was happening, I could clearly see the problem. Yet he couldn't. He was oblivious to the fact it was actually *him*. It doesn't matter how many times you tell someone something, if nothing changes, nothing changes. They say the definition of insanity is doing the same thing over and over again and expecting a different result.

Your job as a leader is not to order others around and pass advice down, but, instead, to meet people where they are and help drag them up. You must discover the skills deficiency in others and use that as kindling for the fire burning within you to share your knowledge. Leaders do not dictate, they educate. This often means your communication style needs to accommodate different learning styles. This requires patience, persistence and a toolbelt of varying skills to help achieve a result. Don't just expect change, work at it. The reason we face these difficulties is not to show people our way of doing things, but, instead, to help discover new solutions that were previously unknown. This is true growth. Give it a shot.

Ideas in Action

Now, if you're wanting to stand out as a Young Leader, we're going to need to develop the idea-generation muscle sitting within your mind. Ideas are the lifeblood of the Young Leader. Without an idea, nothing works, and if you're looking to be an exceptional Young Leader, we need you to step up as the CEO of the idea-creation factory within your mind.

This isn't exclusive to the business owner either. We're always selling. We sell to our boss, our family, our friends and ourselves. Ideas have power. They can *and will* set you apart. Best of all, it only takes one. One idea can completely shift your business, life or way of thinking. But what can we do to ensure their success? Is there a way to help our ideas stand out? Yes, there is, and in this chapter I share my approach with you.

In 1997, when Kevin Roberts first joined the world-leading advertising agency Saatchi and Saatchi as their CEO (a position he held for 19 years), he officially dropped the name 'advertising agency' and decided they would henceforth be known as an 'ideas company'. This was a world first. While most were fighting over the increasingly competitive dollar within 'advertising', K.R. thought differently. Not only did he help the company of 6,500 employees escape the dangers of the red ocean (avoiding the feeding frenzy of supposed competition, fighting for every scrap in the process), but he found an entirely new opportunity inside vast regions of untapped blue ocean available to lead his people into. The question then becomes how you can become your own ideas factory and flex your idea muscle like K.R. did. For this, you'll need to develop your *I.Q.*

Your I.Q.

No, not your *intelligence quotient* (an outdated model of comparing intelligence created by French psychologist Alfred Binet in the early 1900's to help discover children who needed extra 'assistance' to cope with the education system at the time), but your *Idea Quotient*. Your Idea Quotient is based on four key abilities.

1. The ability to know when to **start** an idea
2. The ability to know when to **pitch** an idea
3. The ability to know when to **pivot** an idea
4. The ability to know when to **stop** an idea

Below, I share with you an insight into each one, giving you an insider's look from years of tough learned lessons not just from myself, but also from countless others who have walked before me with an even longer list of lessons.

Starting an idea

The initial genius. Often sparked with a flash of inspiration, this is where it all begins. You need to be aware of these idea-creation moments. Awake to the genius speaking from within that I call your 'Inner Einstein'. Your Inner

Einstein is that feeling of excitement when an idea springs up and you cannot wait to bring it to life. From there, things go one of two ways. You'll either decide to make a go of it and start to bring your idea to life, or you'll allow the fears of your mind to creep in and fill your conscience with all the reasons you *can't* do it. The key to helping your ideas stick is to move to the second stage (pitching your idea) and start testing. As it stands right now, your idea-decision panel has a sample size of just one - you. When put into a real environment, with real customers, your idea will very rarely stand up without some tweaking. Right now, it's still inside your head. Up there, it sounds perfect. Like the next Microsoft, Google or Facebook. As you'll read, however, your idea is still in its most infant form. Like a newborn baby, it might have a heartbeat and some functioning organs, but in its current state it cannot feed itself, let alone stand on its own two feet. It needs to be nurtured. We need it to gather momentum and gain some strength. This is where our second stage comes in: *pitching*.

Pitching an idea

Even though right now your idea exists, it's still extremely volatile. While most believe they need to keep the doors closed and hold the idea close to their chest, I encourage you to do the exact opposite. Your idea needs as much oxygen and light as possible. Rarely will your idea be in its final form and ready to bring to market upon conception. In fact, I'd go as far as saying never. Idea conception is always just the beginning. For an idea to grow, and eventually take off, you need to relentlessly talk about it (pitching). You need to seek feedback from as many qualified people as possible, in as many places as possible and as frequently as possible. You need to live, eat, breathe and sleep the idea.

When I first started developing different ideas, I'd get stuck within the confines of my own mind and shy away from feedback. I'd run with my idea at 100 miles per hour, finish everything I needed and then launch, only to watch as the tumbleweeds drifted by. This was a defence mechanism designed to protect me from the essential (but often shied away from) negative feedback. I'd take the rejection personally and get upset, thinking *I* was the failure. But, as you'll read in the next section, thinking this way will actually kill your idea. Instead, when you're consistently pitching your idea to people, you'll gain much-needed feedback. The more the better. This will progress you to the next stage: *pivoting.*

Pivoting an idea

Most with a scarcity mindset (I've certainly been there) tend to get upset if their idea isn't a smash hit from day one. So what happens when it's not? How can we avoid the constant treadmill of starting again, *again*?

Sometimes all it takes is a simple pivot and switch-up of your approach for your idea to take on a completely new form and serve people in a completely different way. When you can confidently do that, you'll remove the scarcity mindset.

This simple change in trajectory of a few percentage points is often where you can experience extreme growth. I once heard Tiger Woods took eighteen months off professional golf in order to change his swing by just one degree. If one of the world's best golfers can pivot, surely you can too?

Do not make the mistake many make of believing that ideas are static. They're not static - they're progressive. Great ideas change, grow, evolve and, if you're brave enough to let them, take on a life of their own. Yet most idea-creators rarely allow this to happen to their 'baby'. Instead, they put it at extreme risk by smothering it. In reality, the end user will determine which parts of the idea are brilliant and need to stay, and which need to go. Don't get stuck inside your head. Instead, move with your ideas fluidly while keeping their core (*as long as it serves*).

Take Facebook, for example. While it still maintains its core of connecting the world and developing online communities, it has undergone thousands upon thousands of changes during its life as it constantly drives for a greater user experience. Some of those have been major, others are minor. Use your judgement, instinct and intuition to help guide you. This may or may not lead you to the fourth realm: *stopping*.

Stopping an idea

Peter Drucker once wrote "there is nothing so useless as doing efficiently that which should not be done at all." Yet so many get caught up in this trap. What's worse is when they continue doing so, even when they know it's broken. Our ego gets in the way, and we become too proud to stop. There is no shame in stopping. In fact, it takes courage to stop. Often, we become infatuated by the fantasy of what the idea may create rather than the reality of what it is. Instead of separating from the idea, we see the idea as an extension of us. It becomes who we are. And we believe that if it fails, we fail. Here's the thing - you aren't an idea. You're a human. You have many ideas. Some are good, some are bad. Some will serve for a period, others will naturally die. You need to remove the idea from self and stay independent.

This can be done through focusing on the behaviour, seeing that it was perfect in its own way and getting on with things. When you discover there are no mistakes, you can let go of what is holding you back and continue to the next stage of your journey. The quicker you can find what doesn't work, the quicker you'll find the stuff that does. I've lost count of the mistakes I've made, and I haven't even hit 30 yet. But your last mistake is always your best teacher. To move on effectively, objectively identify your actions and accept that they're no longer conducive to your success. At one point in time, this may have been what you wanted, but if it's not producing the result you desire, why continue? Let it go. If you aren't chasing that outcome any longer or have changed your mind, it doesn't make *you* wrong, it was simply the behaviours you exhibited and the actions you took that didn't align with that goal. Make the call. Accept the fact that not all of your ideas will take off, not all of your sales calls will convert, not all of your videos will be watched and not all of your conversations listened to. It's not a reflection of who you are, it's a part of life.

The goal should never be to be perfect in all you do; nor should it be to strive for said perfection (both of those will simply lead to heartache as you miss the impossible targets you've set yourself), but, instead, the goal should simply be to continue chasing an ever greater amount of enjoyment and challenge on your way to reaching your goals, dreams and desires. Always think - progress over perfection.

So keep dreaming new ideas, keep pitching, keep pivoting and keep stopping because the more you focus on what is serving you right now, the more fulfilled you'll ultimately be.

The fifth stage of an idea

There is a fifth stage of an idea that I've been toying with recently in my search to expand my field of vision toward future thinking. One thing I've learned over the past few years is the bigger you can think, the bigger you can act. If you want to be remarkable, you need to create something worthy of being remarked on. And that cannot come from small thinking.

This stage is what I call 50x thinking. It stems back to 2013, when I listened to a book called *The 10X Rule*, written and narrated by the (in)famous Grant Cardone. The entire premise of the book is to not just double or triple your thinking, but to *ten times* your thinking. At the time, it made a lot of sense and I loved the feeling of having my thoughts expanded by ten times.

Then something occurred to me recently. Ironically, it came about while reading my favourite book, *The Magic of Thinking Big* by David S Schwartz. If I could previously expand my thinking to *10x* via Grant Cardone's method, why couldn't I expand it to *20x, 30x* or even *50x*? It takes the same amount of effort, so why not think at that scale? When you ask yourself questions to that level, you get answers on that level. What happens if you 50x what you're doing right now? What level of thinking would that require? What systems would you need in your business or current role? What processes would need to be in place? What would your day to day role look like? How would your life be different? What kind of impact could you create with this level of thinking? It's a seemingly simple exercise, but the effects are profound. Worth taking the time to do for any Young Leader.

Think bigger, dream bigger, act bigger, achieve bigger.

Power of Ask

Sometimes I do stop and reflect on my current life, too. I'm so grateful for the opportunities that have presented themselves along the way. Who would've thought a quiet kid from a small country town would've ever connected with some of the most amazing and highly paid individuals on the planet? Since November 2013, I've had the opportunity to speak with, dine with, interview, be mentored by and spend time with some incredible humans.

I can't take all the credit, though. There is a magic tool that I've been using to achieve this that has never failed me. In fact, it has enabled some of the most life-changing opportunities to occur with minimal downside. I've used it to speak directly (and build important relationships) with millionaires, billionaires, TV stars, elite athletes and hundreds of other experts in their respective fields.

Among them are Jack Canfield (success coach and author of 61 best-selling books, including the *Chicken Soup for the Soul* series which has sold over 500 million copies worldwide); Dr John Demartini (human behavioural specialist who travels the world full time, sharing his methodologies with millions around the globe); Kevin Roberts (former Chairman and CEO of Saatchi and Saatchi - the world's leading ideas company - a position he held for 19 years); Erin Gruwell (the real-life inspiration for the movie: *The Freedom Writers* - one of the best movies you'll ever see; and Josh Phegan (Australia's best and most successful Peak Performance Coach for Real Estate Agents).

Best of all, I've been able to do all the above completely for free. How? By using a little something I call the 'Power of Ask'.

It's quite simple really. So simple, in fact, it's a philosophy you can adopt from this very moment forward. You don't need any particular skill or experience, just a passion to grow and the nous to make it happen. Hopefully you're sitting down for this one. Here it is: *you can have anything you want in this world, if you're just willing to ask.* That's it, just ask. No complicated marketing strategy, or elaborate plan to change the world. Just ask the question.

While most allow their fears to sink in and become paralysed with thoughts of "What if they say no", my response is that sure, they could say no, but what if they say yes? You didn't have it before, and if they say no, you still won't have it, but if they say yes, you *will* have it. No brainer, right?

Now, before you rush off and send those emails, please know the Power of Ask does come with one caveat. It's a major key I learned directly from studying Dr Demartini's work around values. This one thing will most likely determine if you succeed in your requests or are denied.

Discover their Values

Every person on earth has a unique set of personal values. These values are the internal compass we hold that determine what we believe differentiates right from wrong, positive from negative, and opportunity from drawback. Consequently, these values determine how we act, what we believe and how we behave.

It doesn't matter who you are or what you've been through, humans will only ever act in accordance with what they perceive will provide more positive than negative, more upside than downside, more good than bad. Therefore, the key to the Power of Ask (and, in fact, the key to all human communication) is understanding that if you want to get what you want, you must show the desired party how your request will benefit their highest value. The more they can see the link, the greater the chances of an approved request. Your number one goal before you even consider reaching out is to discover what is most important to them.

What do they like?
What do they spend money on?
What do they talk about?
What do they do in their spare time?
What do they surround themselves with?
What information do they share?

Let me share with you a couple of quick examples.

A *teacher's* highest value might be having their work shared. Thus, reaching more people and obtaining more influence is high on their values. A *mother's* highest value might be her children. Thus, keeping those children safe and ensuring a high-quality education for them will be high on her values. An *entrepreneur's* highest value might be new business opportunities. Thus, meeting ambitious people or attending events with other growth-minded individuals will be high on their values.

Speak their language

Once you discover someone's highest values, you hold within yourself a very powerful tool. The key is to take the time to discover what is important to them and what inspires them, and then speak to *that*.

My current top three values are writing, personal growth and teaching. So if someone came to me and started speaking about how to become a New York Times best-selling author, or that they could connect me with a major publisher to get my books into more stores, I am going to become very attentive and open up to that person. I will remember their name and be engaged in what they're saying; I will want to learn more and also want to be close with that person. Conversely, if a new person enters the conversation and switches to the topics of alcohol, reading the newspaper or driving long distances, I will immediately switch off because those topics are very low on my values. However, if that same person spoke to me about a newspaper article from today's paper that mentioned how a famous book agent was in town for one day only who helps emerging authors get onto the New York Times bestsellers list, then I would light up. If they then explained how the agent loved single malt, 17-year-old whiskey, I would head straight to the bottle shop and have a bottle of the finest, single malt, 17-year-old whiskey delivered to their door with a copy of my book. See the difference?

The Secret of Communication

This is the secret that very few get. The key to all communication is *care*. If you don't care enough to take the time to discover what is important to others, you'll be forever frustrated that you can't 'break through' to anyone who doesn't share similar values to you. In an ideal world, you may think you can just be surrounded by those who share your values, but in reality, it just doesn't happen.

Effective communication can be broken into four parts: Knowing what it is you value, caring enough about someone else to discover what is most important to them, understanding how what you're currently doing is serving that person to help them get what they value and, lastly, communicating that in a language they understand. When you do this, you open a dialogue with two sides to the conversation, rather than a monologue where two people are simply waiting for their turn to talk.

As a Young Leader, having this tool inside your toolbelt gives you the head start you need. While 98% of the population never learn this simple truth, you now have the power. Use it wisely, but, more importantly, use it often.

Your Turn

Now it's your turn. Ask yourself, how can I use the Power of Ask, right now? What requests can I make to move further ahead or create opportunities I've been putting off? Who can I open a conversation with? What can I do to help someone else get what they want, while getting what I want?

Then simply follow my foolproof philosophy: no ask - no get. Keep asking, keep trying, keep succeeding. That's the power of asking, and that's what a Young Leader does.

Think different

There is a follow-up to the Power of Ask, however. Besides asking and speaking in their values, you might be wondering how I was able to get on the phone with one of the world's best success coaches, Jack Canfield, for over 90 minutes, completely for free? How about when I was able to get another highly successful coach who travels the world full-time and presents on the same stage as Robin Sharma and Tony Robbins to not only speak on my podcast, but travel 15,556 km to speak to a small group of my coaching clients for the cost of an airfare?

While most send one email and wonder why they never hear back, the Young Leader understands that in order to succeed, it not only takes repeated and consistent efforts, but a strong focus on thinking differently. With no guarantee of success, Young Leaders are willing to try a variety of methods to break through the noise and stand out in a seemingly saturated marketplace. They also understand that while the marketplace may seem saturated, it isn't actually so. Instead, it's filled mostly with those looking for the easy way rather than the one that works. Instead of putting in the hard work, they simply try the same things over and over again.

When I decided I wanted to speak with Jack, not only did I seek out a phone number and call his office, I also sent him (and his sales manager, Teresa) a t-shirt from a movement called 'be nice.' that I created. I then waited six months for that opportunity to come to fruition. Same for my friend JP, who travelled from the other side of the world for me. Both he and his assistant Amanda got a package in the mail. I found a way to stand out and get the most important team member on my side, and did things a little differently to most.

Let me ask, are you prepared to go outside the box? To do the unconventional? Are you standing out amongst the masses and getting in front of the decision makers, while cutting through the noise to share your message directly with those who can make things happen? The moment you move away from regularity and step into the world of crazy, you're putting yourself in pole position. As the late Steve Jobs stated, "it's the ones who are crazy enough to think that they can change the world, are the ones who do." I encourage you - be the crazy one.

Do Hard Things. Often

But alone, just thinking differently is not enough. To be a Young Leader you'll need to be prepared to put in the work and make it happen.

I know you *hear* it all the time. Work hard. Hustle. Grind. 'No Days Off', right? I'm not here to preach to you a series of overused clichés. Those 'success memes' may create virality online but that's as far as they go. Do you want to follow a bunch of empty words placed over a picture of a Lamborghini on a 5-inch screen, or are you here to make a lasting impact on the world? Allow me to let you in on a little secret. To be successful, you need to do hard things. The harder things are, the fewer people will do them. This means you have a huge opportunity to stand out - *if* you're willing to do the work.

Before approaching any project, you need to think not only *how do I become noticed and make my mark,* but also *how can I stay on top?* Becoming successful is one thing; maintaining that success is another. The hardest thing to do once you achieve a specific level of so-called success is stay there. Nothing fails like success. How many times have you seen it? A business reaches the top only to become complacent. Arrogance sets in and they get comfortable. The allure of taking your foot off the gas shows up, and you become tempted to take it easy. I call it 'the success dichotomy'. You work yourself to the bone for success, only to realise the so-called 'success' you've worked for needs to be maintained.

You'll find along your journey that many people love sharing their opinion over what *you* should do with *your* life. This is neither good, nor bad, it's just what they see at the best option for you, and most of the time it actually comes from a place of love.

The thing is, though, unless they truly care to take the time to look at your future goals, desired end game and history, they will simply be recommending options based on their values system.

My advice? Discover what it is you want, and work to bring that to life. Sure, take the advice you get from others on board, but don't subordinate to everyone's opinion. It's up to you to scan, select or scrap the information based on what's relevant for you. Only you know what's best for you. Don't attempt to climb the ladder to success only to discover it's leaning on someone else's wall.

Failure ≠ Defeat

What if you do find yourself in this position, though? Where do you go from here? While most of society would see this as a 'failure', the Young Leader understands it's all a part of the journey. Failure is not only important, it's inevitable. Failure teaches us our toughest, yet most important lessons. Fail fast, learn fast, win fast.

Every successful leader I've ever met shares one thing in common: they've experienced crippling failure. Products that flopped, sales pitches rejected, feelings of giving up that plagued their minds. Sometimes days or weeks at a time. Yet they kept going. This tenacity and ability to stick at things when times are tough is what separates a Young Leader from a young dreamer. It's one of the most difficult things you will experience on your journey. When these feelings come (and they will come), you need to know something. You are not alone. What you are going through is completely normal. I've spoken to some of the most successful people on earth and also people just like you and me. We all experience times of self-doubt and confusion. But, as I've stated in earlier chapters, embracing the confusion and using it as fuel is the key. Take solace in the fact that no matter who you are, what you do or where you come from, at some point you're going to fail. Yet also know that with every failure comes a valuable lesson, and every setback brings you closer to your goal. Keep searching for your path; you will find it.

One life at a time

Before you continue your pursuit of excellence, however, I need to share something with you. As you walk the earth, you'll find many claiming they will change the world. Yet very few are able to follow through. They read a generic marketing book telling them they need to create a mission statement that stands out and helps them become noticed: "Our mission is to change 10,000 lives", or "We won't stop until we impact 1 million people", the overly optimistic words state. Yet why do so few achieve such a result?

Before sharing a 'dream' of changing 10,000 lives, I have to ask, can you confidently state you have changed *one* life? Have you provided something truly remarkable that has completely shifted *one* person's thinking, situation and outlook on life? Overhauled their entire existence? If not, it's where you need to start.

With every person I coach, mentor or help, my goal is to imagine placing a 'tick' next to their name on the 'lives changed' list contained within my head. To leave each life better than how I found it. Young Leaders work at giving maximum value, to help impact one person at a time and share a new perspective with them. The world isn't changed through some grandiose mission statement, but, instead, through the process of changing one life at a time. Who's on your list, and what will it take to put a tick next to their name?

PART 3: SHINE BRIGHT

Okay, now we have you showing up and standing out, it's time to share the third level of becoming a Young Leader: *Shining Bright.*

For years I shied away from my story. I kept quiet and hid my voice. I stayed small because I believed I was just like everyone else.

Shining bright is about finding that inner champion and becoming your own biggest fan. To discover that voice from within to share your unique story with the world. This is what I share with you over the following pages. I also show you how to start taking massive action upon your dreams before sharing with you a strategy to use to increase your impact. People buy how you think - best to make sure that thinking is different to the rest. Lastly, I provide some practical insights into the world of energy. Let's finish strong, shine bright like summer and prepare for take-off.

Become Your Own Biggest Fan

As you climb your ladder to success, you'll find many willing to support you, many willing to tear you down and many who, quite frankly, don't care either way.

There is one person, however, who will constantly be there throughout this entire journey. They live in your house. They're with you while you sleep. They're there first thing in the morning and last thing at night. They know what you're struggling with, and what you're proud of. They hear everything you say and see everything you do. This person is, of course, *you*.

As a Young Leader, the hardest person you'll ever have to face is the one staring back at you from the mirror. The self-talk that goes on inside that 3-pound mass between those two ears of yours can have a major effect on your mood, success, outlook and attitude. It can make you or it can break you. It can be your biggest fan or your fiercest competitor. Your best friend or your worst enemy. It can support you or it can bring you down. It knows when you start a goal where it will pump you up and get you excited about the possibilities, and also knows when you're close to achieving that goal so it can chime in with some self-doubt and negative language just for you. Sometimes you'll love it; other times you'll hate it. But what I've realised is that no matter what, in some way, shape or form, this voice serves.

Your Inner Bully

For years, I was what my good friend, Jean-Pierre De Villiers, would call 'my own worst bully'. All day I would inspire others, while internally tearing myself down. I would speak positive things of others, while viewing myself as worthless. I would constantly be in a state of confusion, while believing others had some magic key I didn't. The result of all of this? *A lot* of negative self-talk equipped with feelings of low self-esteem, and low confidence. The self-talking demon was out in full force.

Eventually I got tired of the constant head games and knew something had to be done. Yet it's never easy. As leaders, we stand out in front, knowing our tribe is waiting behind us, trusting we make the right move. *What if I make the wrong call? What if I go the wrong way? Make a mistake?* The thoughts can be paralysing.

Yet attempting to live with the goal of never making a mistake is an unrealistic demand. We all make mistakes - it's what helps us learn. The more we attempt not to, the more we dig ourselves deeper into the hole.

Ironically, guess who is placing this perfect expectation upon you? *You.* We strive to never be wrong, yet the reality is that no-one is right 100% of the time. Yes, as a leader you're here to guide, help and assist as much as you can, but people need to take full responsibility for themselves. You're doing the best you can, with what you've got. You may be forging a new path, but that also means you're the first to face the many challenges encountered along the way.

While it's easy to think our tribe won't understand these challenges, the reality is, it's the exact opposite. Those we support are looking for ways to support us in return. It may not be in the same form, but in some way, they're happy to give back to the person giving themselves for the group.

We don't normally see it like this, though. Instead, we continually place an increasing demand upon ourselves under the belief that we have to weather the storm alone, otherwise we may be perceived as weak or a failure. Newsflash: it doesn't have to be this way. You don't have to have all the answers. None of us do (nor do we need to).

The job of the leader is not to be flawless and never make a mistake, but instead to put themselves on the frontline and make mistakes *on behalf* of those they lead so as to reduce the amount of stress for them. Whether you like it or not, you're a flawed human being, just like the rest of us.

At some point, I guess we all need reminding of that, though. Just because we face the fear doesn't make it any easier. At times, we all feel the doubt and uncertainty that comes with the honour of leadership, but that's what we signed up for. If you're not up for it, there are plenty of places back in victim-land. But you and I both know there is no turning back now.

Removing Your Inner Bully

So what can we do? The good news is that recognition is the first step toward 'recovery'. Once we've recognised the situation, we can work on a brighter future. We do this through acknowledgement of our achievements. Whether you're aware of it or not, over the years you've done some truly remarkable things. Maybe you've completed high school or obtained a university degree. Maybe you're good at a particular sport or have a passion for something unique. Even having the ability to read, write or speak is a major achievement. As time goes on, however, these achievements seem increasingly insignificant. Do you know how proud your parents were when you took your first steps? What about riding your bike without training wheels for the first time? Even falling off didn't stop you. And what about swimming without drowning? At one point in your life, these were all monumental. You were born with *none* of these skills. In fact, when you were born, you couldn't even support your own head. Now, though, you have more than enough strength for that, along with a huge list of achievements compiled and amassed from the very moment you entered this world.

As humans, though, we naturally tend to discount our own achievements and fall into the comparison trap. We see others and view them as *above us* and, in doing so, we lose our power. *Sure, I can do 'that', but it is nothing compared to what 'they' can do,* touts our Inner Bully.

Remember, they are them, and you are you. Neither is more special or less special, nor is one more important or less important: we're all simply travelling our own path on the journey of life. We've all had our own challenges, as well as our own lucky breaks. And we've all been gifted with an incredible power to change the world, too.

However, when stuck in the comparison trap, you won't be able to see it. You're stuck in your own head. As Tony Robbins says, "If you stay in your head, you're dead". You need to get out of this cycle to allow you to see your own brilliance. One incredible way to do this is through an exercise I learned from Dr John Demartini.

Firstly, discover who it is you're comparing yourself to and write their name down, as well as the exact behaviour you're comparing yourself to. Be as specific as possible. It could be financial business success, unique customer service, incredible fitness capacity or specialised knowledge in a particular area.

Next, I want you to write a situation in which you were perceived by others to show the exact same behaviour, and who saw it. The more the better. Continue listing situations and names until you have absolute certainty that you have displayed the exact same behaviour, to the exact degree as the person to whom you previously compared yourself. This will be hard - really hard. But by doing this thoroughly, I promise you, you'll be able to remove feelings of self-doubt and comparison, while also awakening the genius sitting inside.

I did this recently with one of my clients. She was stuck comparing herself to a mentor who was a genius in the human body and had specialised knowledge in that area.

Little did she know, she too was a genius in that area, and I was about to wake that up within her.

For 90 minutes, we sat and brainstormed all the times she too had displayed specialised knowledge of the human body, and listed all the people who had seen it or been impacted by her amazing gift. We filled pages and pages with situations and names. I could literally see her face change as she discovered she had the exact same level of genius within. The penny dropped.

After her shift, we worked our way down the list and (conservatively) estimated all the people she had impacted through her specialised knowledge of the human body. As she read the numbers out, I typed them into the calculator on my phone. *Fifty, thirty, seven, a thousand.* On and on we went, until the last one. I turned my phone screen around and showed her the number. 31,726. "Thirty-one thousand, seven hundred and twenty-six people are now better off because of your specialised knowledge of the human body," I shared with her. Knowing she grew up in a town of 3,000 people, I asked her what it felt like to know she had impacted over ten times the population of the very town she grew up in. She was speechless. I then asked her if she felt like a genius in the area of specialised knowledge of the human body. Her answer? *"Absolutely"*.

Later that night she sent me a thank-you message stating she couldn't believe what had happened. I could, though. My certainty exceeded her doubt. I knew there was a genius sitting inside, waiting to be awoken. All we had to do was remove the block within to unlock her power.

The battle of comparison is one you simply cannot win. Instead, embrace the path you've already walked and begin to appreciate yourself for the brilliant miracle you are. You were not put on this earth to constantly be in a state of confusion or comparison. You were here to shine bright. There are no other you's like you. Stop being your own worst enemy and start being your own best friend. Flick the switch today and let's unlock your hidden genius.

Your Story is Your Strength, Your Pain is Your Power

As I've mentioned to you a couple of times earlier, I was pretty shy growing up (even left my year 10 formal after being there for two hours because I don't particularly like large crowds or the party environment). On top of that, I was repeatedly told I ask too many questions and that I should just keep quiet. At one point I was even dubbed "Quey" (short for questions) for my inquisitive nature.

For years, I thought there must be something wrong with me. Why did I always ask so many questions? This constant self-appraisal literally stopped me from being me. But the moment I stopped hiding from my inquisitive nature and embraced my 'question asking', things changed dramatically. Not only have I interviewed hundreds of amazingly successful people (while sharing it with hundreds of thousands of others), but it's also allowed me to create a business where I get to share my love for learning with other inquisitive question askers. In fact, my entire business has been built around building inspirational events and asking great questions. I simply ask the right questions of the right people and *voila*, like magic, my pain becomes my power and my story becomes my strength.

What has happened in your past is extremely powerful and makes you, you. Ask yourself, how can I turn my story into a strength and transform my pain into power?

What amazing things have happened during my life? What challenges have I faced? Where have I been? Or not been (*yet*)? Who has helped me? Who has hindered me? Why do I do what I do? What made me decide to do that? What message do I want to share? What was my first job like? Write it all down. Get it all out.

What you're going to find is that no-one else on earth has been fortunate enough to experience the unique things you have. And I say 'fortunate' fully understanding the fact that, at times, things may have been tough. Really tough. Thing is, we've all been through hard times, but what I want you to focus on is the hidden blessing within. They say the best gifts often come poorly wrapped. If you're stuck allowing the experiences from your past to control you, ask yourself, how did they serve me? What opportunities were created because of them? How did they progress my thinking? How did I grow from them? How would things be had they *not* happened?

Don't let perceived negative experiences have control over you. Instead, draw power from them and use them as fuel for the future. Everything has happened to you for a reason, and everything has an upside. It just needs to be found.

Finding your Greatness

It reminds me of the campaign *Find Your Greatness* created by Nike in 2012 (worth looking up when you get a chance). The clip shows everyday athletes (Nike's philosophy is 'everyone is an athlete') displaying everyday acts of courage while doing what they love. It shows them taking the hits, putting in the work and getting the job done - whether there is an audience or not. A voice speaks over the clip explaining Nike's belief around 'greatness' which I had to share with you:

Greatness. It's just something we made up. Somehow, we've come to believe that greatness is a gift, reserved for a chosen few. For prodigies. For superstars. And the rest of us can only stand by, watching.

You can forget that. Greatness is not some rare DNA strand. It's not some precious thing. Greatness is no more unique to us than breathing. We're all capable of it - all of us.

The ad continues:

Greatness needs a lot of things, but it doesn't need an audience.

And

Greatness is not born, it's made.

Love it. Some brands just get it. Nike is one of them. While most shove their crazy prices, discount deals and super sales down your throat, Nike marches to a different beat - its own beat. It inspires from within. No matter who you are, where you're from or what you look like, it makes you believe.

This is what I want for you. I want you to find your greatness. That special feeling from within where you cannot wait to do something. The one where you can't sleep at night because you're excited thinking of the possibilities. It gets you up in the mornings (even during winter) and keeps you up at night. It does exist, and you will find it.

How can I be so sure? Because I'm feeling it right now. For the past four years, every single day I've shared my writing in some form. And for the past eight months I've braved the morning at 3:50 am five days a week to write uninterrupted in order to put these words together and share my passion with you. My greatness is sharing this message.

There is nothing on earth more powerful than having access to this state. When working from within, challenges are recognised for what they are (simply speed bumps along the way), doubt dissipates, our confidence reigns supreme and we become unstoppable. Let's find your greatness and make the impossible, possible.

While many discount their story or hide from it completely, leaders own it. Now it's your turn. Own your story; it's made you who you are. Draw power from your pain; it's built your strength. And embrace the tough times because that's where you've learned the best lessons. Enjoy the ride. We only get one shot.

Talk Big, Act Bigger

Sometimes, though, as a seeker, you'll find your mind running wild with dreams, possibilities and aspirations. Because of this passion, we cannot wait to share them. However, most will tell you not to vocalise them. "Keep it close" or "Show, don't tell", they claim. I do not agree. I love sharing mine. I tell the world and become accountable to not just myself, but to as many people as possible. There is nothing I love more than saying I'm going to do something and then doing it...nothing. The Young Leader shines bright with enthusiasm and takes every opportunity to talk about what they love.

Along this journey, however, you'll find no shortage of excuse makers, who are ready (and willing) to cut down your dreams. These 'Dream Takers' want to keep you small. That way, they feel less insecure about themselves for not living up to the potential they know lies deep within. The knowing that if they were asked "Did I do all I could with all I had?" on their deathbed, the answer would unfortunately be "no".

Do not let them project their fears onto you. While most attempt to hide from their fears, shoving them deeper and deeper into the corners of the mind where only they know where to find them, the Young Leader faces theirs. The Young Leader understands that if they're not currently on target for where they want to be, it's up to them to fix it.

Your Potential Self

This gap that exists between where you currently are and where you know deep down you could be is called the 'Potential Gap'. The only way to close this gap is through your 'Potential Self' taking the leap and crossing the chasm.

Our 'Potential Self' is our inner dreamer. The one with a childlike hunger for creativity and an unquenchable thirst for knowledge. Our 'Potential Self' doesn't get self-conscious or intimidated by change; nor does it fear rejection or failure. In fact, our 'Potential Self' lives in a world of abundance, rich with opportunity. And even though at any given point there may still be unfulfilled hopes, dreams and desires, it maintains a burning desire to continue growing as it knows this is our true purpose on Planet Earth. Our 'Potential Self' is the ultimate seeker. And while your journey certainly won't be challenge-free, the challenges experienced along the way will be recognised for what they are: life's greatest lessons. Our grand purpose here is to be more of our 'Potential Self' and close the gap toward our full potential.

It does, however, raise the question: how do we escape the prison our fears are holding us captive in and live life completely on our terms? Is it even possible? Absolutely. Is it easy? Not always.

You're going to need to stop playing small, develop the confidence necessary to step out of the shadows of darkness and make the decision to go all in with life.

Who Do You Think You Are?

Right here is where most will scare themselves out of even getting started, though. They see themselves as so far from their goal that it's virtually impossible to jump in the driver's seat of their perfect life. Please know that if it weren't possible, your mind would not be showing it to you. Our conscious (and subconscious) mind will never allow us to see anything that isn't on some level possible. So instead of sitting there complaining or playing victim, wouldn't it be wiser to put in the work and start to make it happen?

Despite what most will try to tell you, they actually don't want to change. I have learned to take little notice of what people say, and much more of what they do. Actions never lie. A lot of people will continue to do the same thing, yet foolishly expect a different result or for things to magically work out. Do you see anything wrong with that logic?

Here's the thing about change: it's hard, it's scary, it's unknown and the very thought of it can be all consuming. It's why 99.99% of people will never change to the extent they truly could. Proper change requires you to shift to a new paradigm and forces you to give up your excuses (something most aren't prepared to do).

It's the thought of poking their head into the rabbit hole and not knowing what they might see that scares most people out of ever exploring anything other than their current reality. If only they would open their mind. The world would reveal the reality of how small they are truly playing, while opening their eyes to vast possibilities. You either want it, or you don't.

Now, if you do, the best place to start is by taking the action steps required towards becoming who you need to become in order to live the life you're envisaging. What kind of conversations would this person have? Who would they hang around? What thoughts would they think and what daily actions would they take? Would they be focused on what could go wrong and the negative aspects of their life? Or would they be continually searching for options and looking at how each and every situation brings with it a new opportunity for growth?

The Strangest Secret

This is the strangest secret within the entire world of achievement. While most are searching for the latest gimmick to reach their goal, faster, easier and quicker, the Young Leader understands that the primary purpose of setting a goal is not about reaching the destination, but, instead, about the person they become along the way to achieving that goal. To paraphrase success guru Earl Nightingale, "success is not a destination, but instead, the progressive realisation of a worthy ideal".

While most spin their wheels endlessly for the supposed gold at the end of the rainbow, the Young Leader understands the true gold is collected along the way.

Dream Out Loud

But you can't do it alone. If you're going to make a go of this thing we call life, it's crucial you share your mission with as many people as you can. The more you do, the more others will be drawn toward helping you. The clearer you are on what it is you want, the more you're going to continually attract people, experiences and opportunities that further your progress along the way. Some will be there to provide support; others will be there to provide challenge. Those supporting will show up when you're about to give up, and those who challenge you will show up when you are off track and need your course corrected. Both serve, and both will help you grow.

One of my favourite lines inside one of my favourite books, *The Alchemist* by Paulo Coelho, states "when you want something, all the universe conspires in helping you to achieve it." Couldn't be more true. To achieve big, you need to set big goals and get vocal with them. Tell your family, tell your friends and tell the universe. Then go out into the world and make it happen. You were not put on this earth just to work, eat, sleep and die.

You are capable of so much more. At any given point, most are really only living 5% of their true potential, yet once we discover our true purpose and mission, we're able to open up the other 95%. But we're only ever shown what this 95% looks like when working toward our highest purpose.

True Inspiration

The more we focus on that which is truly important to us, the more fulfilment we ultimately feel. When we work toward that which is aligned with our highest values, we cannot help but raise our self-esteem and confidence. Best of all, while doing so, not only do we derive pleasure, but we actually seek out challenge too - sometimes consciously, while other times, unconsciously. We do this in order to generate and spawn new growth. Despite the feeling of discomfort that can often accompany growth, when we're truly inspired and working toward our highest purpose, this won't be seen as negative, but, instead, be welcomed, as it means more growth.

You are so brilliant in your very own way. The pure genius you exhibit when working from true inspiration is unrivalled. Every single one of us has that one thing within us that makes our eyes light up and our heart beat faster. When we do it, we lose time and become the activity. Nothing else seems to matter, and we become untouchable.

Yet years of conditioning, belittlement and judgement from others, usually only considering their own wants and desires, means we're often clouded as to what we truly love. We minimise ourselves to their expectations and shrink our power. We allow their expectations and limitations to creep in and, as a result, we lose our spark. Time to get it back. Time to get you back.

(Re)Inspire

Think about what it is you love more than anything else in this world. Imagine yourself doing this activity with zero distraction. You have no other worries. No bills, no fighting with the family, no time limits. Completely free. Limitless. Just the best version of you, simply doing what you love and loving what you do.

Allow yourself to become lost in the moment. Recall the feeling of having discovered it for the first time, the moment you knew it was difficult but also the moment you knew you wanted to master it. Recall how much you loved it, even when your family and friends were tired of you talking about it. Recall that feeling of not wanting to wait to do it again (and again and again).

Take a moment to just sit and observe yourself here. Look at the smile on your face, observe the environment around you and feel what it feels like to be here. Push the oxygen right into the bottom of your stomach and breathe deep. Feel your stomach expand and contract with each breath.

This is what true inspiration feels like. Imagine what you could achieve if you worked from this place every day. What would be possible if you played at this level? Not just today, or tomorrow, but what would happen if for the next 12 months you embraced this same focus, energy and passion? How about the next five years? Or forty? Does it inspire you? Good. Does it scare you? Also good. That means it's truly what you wish to bring into the world.

Inspiration is something every single person on this planet is capable of. It's part of the human experience - and something we all deserve. Yet, sadly, not all of us have a say in the matter. Some are forced to work from three years old just to survive; some are pushed into studying what their parents want and end up in a job they hate, and some are born into a life filled with things they don't even like, even if they're good at them (look up Andre Agassi if you want to know more about that one).

The good news is, if you're reading this, chances are you do have a choice. For some, that may be a little hazy right now, but trust me, you do. You can either choose to continue living a mediocre life for another 30, 40, 50+ years before dying with a life filled with deep regret and the pain of missed opportunity, or you can make the choice right here, right now, that you're going to be among the rare few who act upon their dreams. The slim percentage who execute, rather than excuse themselves. While most are paralysed waiting for the right time, perfect opportunity, beginning of a new year or the planets to align, you can get a head start and begin to fulfil your current purpose from this very moment on.

Imagine a world where everyone worked from that level of greatness every day of their lives? Can it be done? Yes - that I am sure of. But it starts one person at a time. And if it's going to happen in our lifetime, we're going to need you to step up to the plate and be that person...today.

Decide today that you're going to live boldly and become the leader you know you can be. In times of great uncertainty, you can be the shining beacon of hope so many desperately need. Stop sabotaging yourself, and give yourself permission to be great. Stop waiting; it starts now.

Don't Save Anything For The Trip Back

But how? How do you develop such a hunger from within that no matter what, you decide to keep going? To ride through the storm even when you're scared and alone, and have no idea which way to go?

The only way to do this is by going all in. Success and effective leadership demand you go all in. To burn the boats and never look back.

There's a scene in the movie *Gattaca* that showcases perfectly the lengths one person will go to achieve their dreams. During the entire film, the main character, Vincent, is tested - both physically and mentally. In a world in which he doesn't belong, he shows us the sacrifice necessary to make his dreams a reality.

Throughout the movie, Vincent and his brother Anton (a genetically modified perfect specimen) play a game they call 'chicken'. They'll swim endlessly into the ocean until one is too 'chicken' to keep going and gives up to head back to shore. When they played, Anton, the smarter, stronger brother spawned from both his mother and father's 'perfect' genes, would always win.

Except once. On one occasion the movie shows a time when Vincent had to rescue Anton from drowning. It's the only edge his inferior brother has ever had over him. It makes for a perfect climactic scene towards the end of the movie where, late into the night, Anton challenges Vincent to one last game of chicken.

In the dark of the night, they take off their jackets, ties and pants in preparation for the swim ahead. Both brothers have no idea what is to transpire, but both are too proud to back down. The waves crash heavily against the surrounding rocks while the moonlight provides the scene with just enough light to see what is happening. They enter the freezing water before swimming stroke for stroke into the ocean.

Eventually, Anton calls out to his brother, "Vincent. Where's the shore?" Vincent responds, "You want to quit....?" "NO!" comes the reply. The two continue into the ocean before Anton once again calls out to his brother, "Vincent! How are you doing this, Vincent? How have you done any of this? We have to go back." Vincent replies hastily, "It's too late for that. We're closer to the other side." "What other side! You want to drown us both?" shouts Anton. "You want to know how I did it? This is how I did it, Anton...I never saved anything for the swim back," reveals Vincent, before staring at his brother with a look of pure determination. For Vincent, it's victory or death. Realising this, Anton decides to concede defeat before making his way back to the shore (although not before temporarily drowning on the way back, where his supposedly inferior brother, Vincent, must once again save him).

"I never saved anything for the swim back." I still get goosebumps when I hear that line. Powerful scene. Just goes to show hard work beats talent and genetics, every time.

I'll occasionally take new coaching clients out for a run during one of our first meetings. I take them to a track near my house which is around four kilometres and includes a brutal hill at the end. I only have one rule - do not save anything for the trip back. It's astounding what this attitude does. It transforms thinking and transcends limits. It doesn't just tell you to believe, it helps you feel it.

While most save a little in reserve for their 'trip back', imagine if you took the same approach as Vincent and went all in. If you stopped at nothing and put it all on the line, fully knowing you have no idea how far away the other side is.

I think you know what needs to be done. Time to kill. Now get out there and achieve big; I've got your back.

Build Your Army

So now I've shared with you some deep insights and a pathway to becoming a Young Leader, I can hear you asking *where do I begin? How do I get myself out there? Where's the starting line and how do I have the impact I desire with no 'name'? After all, who would want to listen to* me*?*

Turns out, a lot of people. Inspiration is contagious, and to impact the world on the level we need you to, sitting idle is not an option. You have an obligation to share what you love, and I want to see you spread it like wildfire.

While most at this stage will retreat into their comfort zones and allow fear to take control, my hope for you is that the words within this book have helped inspire you to move beyond this state and allowed you to see the possibilities that lie ahead for the Young Leader who has made the decision that nothing will get in their way.

Once that decision has been made, however, you'll need two things: strategy and firepower. This is what I want to share with you in this chapter. I call it 'Building Your Army', and it's the single most powerful way I know to find your voice, share it with the world and grow your impact.

Finding Your Voice

We start with a focus on finding your voice. You can have the right message, at the right time, but if you aren't sharing it effectively, it's going to be wasted. The voice you use when sharing your message is just as important as the message itself.

Allow me to share an example from two coaches I know. Let's call them Jim and Tim. Jim is focused on delivering specific, relevant and timely content to his audience. He focuses on the specific things that inspire others and can help move someone forward effectively, while using high-quality video within a quiet environment.

Tim, on the other hand, chooses to go on 'Sunday Night Rants'. He shoots these from his home office on a mobile phone while swearing, screaming and yelling down the camera lens at all the things he sees wrong with the world.

Neither is right or wrong, and both are very popular in their own way. While I personally resonate with Jim's message and much prefer to consume his content, every Sunday night people religiously tune into Tim's 'Sunday Night Rants' and rave about his passion. Both have found their voice. A way to penetrate the noise and cut through to the consumer.

When we first discover something we become passionate about, we love to share it - that's the good news. The not so good news is sometimes we don't really know who to share it with, how to get it out there or even what 'style' to use. Do we want to be Jim or Tim?

What usually happens is we end up sharing it in the same way we heard it and basically parrot it to anyone who will listen. Now emulation isn't necessarily a bad thing, and in the early stages of your growth, it'll be how you share your message (because you won't know any other way). However, to lead others, as soon as you can you'll need to find your unique voice. This will allow you to share *your* message, *your* way.

But how? One word - *practice*. Finding your voice takes time, and the only way to discover it is by doing. Sorry - there isn't a manual for that, nor is there a three-step guide. You'll have to perform the reps yourself.

Back in 2015 I did a Facebook Live video every day for 12 weeks. At the time, I was reading around a book a week, and I wanted to share the wisdom I was gaining while also solidifying the lessons within my head. That, and I knew I wanted to get better on video (find my voice).

So Monday to Friday I would jump on video, in front of a whiteboard, to an audience of five (hey, we all start somewhere), and I'd share a summary from the books I was reading.

The point of this was not to try and build my name, but, instead, to push me to find my voice. By going live I was forced to think on my feet and fully commit. The thought of social embarrassment (which was inevitable and happened multiple times throughout) drove me to improve.

But what I found was the person who delivered their message on day 1 was completely different by day 84. The 'voice' (and style) had completely changed. Instead of being rigid and uptight, I was a lot more relaxed and fluent. Instead of rushing and stumbling, I took my time and delivered the content more succinctly.

This same philosophy goes for my podcast, and also my writing. When I first started, both were pretty shocking. But now, after 150+ episodes of the podcast and four years of daily writing, it's all a distant memory.

And now I want that for you. But it won't just happen. To make a difference, you'll need two things. 1. You'll need to put yourself out there and practise. 2. You'll need to focus each time on small, daily improvements. It doesn't matter where you start, only that you're making progress.

Set yourself a challenge like I did. Force yourself to grow, expand and find your voice. It will take practice and in the beginning, it will be uncomfortable. But if you stick with it, you'll find what works. Trust the process and jump in.

Find Your Vehicle

Next, we need to help you find a vehicle to use to share your passion with the world. As you might have picked up so far from this guide, you are unique. You have specific skills and specialised knowledge, and have lived through certain experiences that no-one else on this earth has. Yet unless you have a big enough reason to share it with the world, it's forever going to stay within you.

Right now, there are so many ways for you to share what you love with us. The internet and commoditisation of data has made this very easy. The power has been given to the people. Every single one of us is now our very own media company. Podcasting is the new radio. Facebook is the new newspaper. YouTube is the new TV. And best of all, you can use all the above to broadcast yourself and your story across the world, completely for free.

I imagine every piece of content I release as a soldier in my digital army. Every time I post a new video, I have another little soldier out in the world fighting for my cause. Every time I post a new blog, I have another soldier out on the battlefield doing great things for me. Every time I gift someone a 'be nice.' t-shirt or release a new podcast, or someone downloads a piece of content I've created, I get closer to my goal through the work of my army. Best of all, they do it at scale. Twenty-four hours a day, seven days a week, my army is working relentlessly for me to impact those who need it most. Even this little book you hold is working hard for me.

Never in a million years would I have thought that hundreds of thousands of people would want to hear my thoughts, questions and ideas. Yet every day, they tune into my podcast, watch my videos, read my blogs, seek out my advice and, like you, read my book. My soldiers are doing their job and spreading my message.

Create > Consume

Now it's your turn. I challenge you to look within and find your inner gold. Discover what makes you, you. Instead of minimising yourself to others and consuming *their* content, I want *you* to be the creator. To build *your* army. To find *your* platform and share *your* story with the world. Your thoughts and outlook on life.

I want to listen to *your* podcast, watch *your* videos, read *your* blog and hold *your* book. It's time for you to release your soldiers onto the battlefield and help others grow. Time to share your mistakes, lessons and unique story. Because the truth is, while it's stuck within you, it's not helping anyone. When it's stuck in that overthinking mind of yours, it's useless. We need to draw it out. Get all those problems, fears and frustrations you've had along the way out and into a format that can ultimately serve others.

Now more than ever, people are craving unique stories. Stories help us connect and right now you have the opportunity to share yours with the world. My hope for you is that you take action on this and share the gift of you with the world. It's liberating, empowering and extremely rewarding. The best inspiration comes from action, and you have no idea just how much impact you can have simply by sharing 'you'.

Yes, it takes courage and yes, it puts you in a vulnerable position, but that's what being a leader is all about. The best leaders lead by example and allow those who believe they do not yet have the courage to see they actually do. By living in your greatness, standing on the shoulders of giants rather than in their shadows and sharing yourself out on the ledge of life, you give others permission to do the same. That's leadership. That's true power. And that's the world I want to live in. Get started releasing your soldiers today and before you know it, you'll have an entire army behind you fighting for your cause.

Endless Energy

As we draw to a close, in this last chapter I want to share with you some simple yet powerful insights on not only how you can perform at your peak year-round, but also how you can avoid near certain burnout if you aren't following the rules of the game. What I'm talking about here is energy, and how it relates to us as humans.

For years, I believed the only forms of energy that existed were simply physical and emotional. Yet recently I discovered there are actually four realms of energy in and around us that all top leaders understand:

1. Physical Energy
2. Emotional Energy
3. Mental Energy
4. Spiritual Energy

At its core, everything on this earth is energy. How you feel, how you act, how you make decisions, how you move, how you communicate. All that is around you, above you, beside you and beneath you. Everything.

Unlike time, which is finite, energy is a renewable resource. Yet most don't understand this seemingly hidden benefit, let alone take advantage of it. Most run their batteries to zero, before charging back to 50% and once again forcing themselves to hit the road at a hundred miles per hour.

Inside this chapter I explain what each of these mean, along with some simple methods to ensure you're full of *energy* when you need it.

Realities

Many talk about burnout; few actually experience it. (Un)fortunately, I've been there. Working two jobs and accumulating 110 hours per week with four hours sleep each night left just a few hours left over for anything else (and trust me, there wasn't much I felt like doing; it's no way to live). Besides the workload and destructive self-behaviour, your entire life crumbles around you. But not right away. For a while, most around you will appreciate and admire your work ethic. Then, like anything out of balance, things will start to fall apart. Your partner will start to get frustrated because you're never 'present'. While you claim that you're 'with them', you know deep down that while your body might be, your mind isn't. Your family will notice you're increasingly distant and disengaged. Your work quality will suffer, and you'll start to feel more and more burnt out. Sex drive? Gone. Productivity? Gone. Desire for anything other than work? Gone. You become numb, and nothing seems to matter. And for what? To wear as a badge of honour?

Endless Optimisation

We chase a life of endless optimisation, only to dig our own grave deeper and deeper. For years, I didn't watch movies because it 'wasted time'. When my friends asked if I'd seen any movies lately, I'd proudly reply "No, I don't have time for movies". *Man, Hayden must be so busy*, I imagined they thought. Made me feel kind of good, you know?

To be honest, though, it's the work of our biggest enemy - the ego. The ego craves attention and recognition. It feeds off empty 'likes' on social media and encourages you to be superhuman, without wanting to deal with the consequences of such behaviour. Sustaining this, though, just isn't possible. I cannot guarantee you a formula for success, but I know the formula for failure, and it's attempting to live a perfect life.

For years, this is how I lived my life. I spent every waking moment as though I had to cram my brain with more 'information' in the hopes of being more productive. I wouldn't let a minute go by where I wasn't listening to an audiobook or a podcast. I wouldn't go out because I'd need to finish the busy work I'd created for myself. I'd stay up late and get up early. I refused to be 'still'. Yet only now am I starting to see the benefits of doing so. Lately, I've 'allowed' myself to take some time out to watch movies again. In doing so, I've been exposed to some really amazing and thought-provoking moments through the screen. It's certainly been helping me connect with something bigger. Call it spiritual, or a higher power if you like (just labels), but the more I stand back and see life for what it really is, the more I see that the entire pursuit of a perfectly optimised existence, that I used to attempt to live, is an unwinnable battle.

I'm not here to preach anything to you, and I'm certainly still a work in progress, but my hope for you here today is to simply offer you solace into another way of thinking. If you're trapped inside this same cycle, just know, there is a way out.

Zoom Out

It's hard to see the bigger picture while you are 'in it', but I'd like you to attempt to pause for just a second, zoom out and imagine the performance and output you could achieve if you were able to recharge back to 100% each day and reach your full capacity. Even if you think you're productive right now, when you're constantly 'on', you're doing yourself and everyone around you a disservice. You wouldn't run a Ferrari at 14,000 RPM's 24/7, so why would you do it to your mind, body and spirit?

My goal here is not to transform you to leap out of bed every morning with boundless energy - that's an unrealistic ideal created by self-help authors in an attempt to sell more books - but I do believe you can maximise your output and achieve a dramatic increase in results with just a few simple, yet powerful changes (oh, and getting out of bed will actually be a lot easier).

Stress and Renewal

In order to make it happen, though, you need to understand the two key abilities of peak performance:

1. Your ability to stress

2.   Your ability to renew

The higher both of these metrics are, the greater your capacity. The greater your capacity, the higher your efficiency. Like anything, though, we need a mix of both stress and renewal to maximise results (with stress needing to be slightly increased each time, thus helping you build your capacity).

Thing is, most people are either over-training and under-renewing (too much stress) or under-training and over-renewing (not enough stress). Both lead to imbalances and reduced performance, thus causing subpar results. So what can we do?

The Two R's

Allow me to introduce you to my two friends: 'Routines' and 'Rituals'. The two R's that will set you free. Routines help you run at your highest capacity, without draining too much brain battery power (explained below), while Rituals help energise you to recover bigger, stronger, more efficiently and at a faster rate to recharge that same battery.

Routines Explained

The reason Routines work so well is because of our finite decision making power. I call this our 'brain battery power'. Just like a regular battery, each day we are given a certain amount of charge to go out into the world and perform tasks. Despite the number of choices most believe they're asked to make per day, it's actually a lot higher (estimates suggesting 35,000+ decisions every single day). Thing is, each time we're asked to make a choice, it takes a certain amount of 'decision-making' power. This causes our brain battery to slightly drain. Another decision, another small drain. Routines allow you to streamline certain decisions and save your power for the decisions and tasks that really matter.

Albert Einstein, Steve Jobs and Barack Obama all respectively wore the exact same style of clothing each day. They understood that every decision had a crucial impact on their brain battery. The more they could reduce the drain on insignificant things such as what to wear, the more power they had for monumental decisions that could impact the world. I'm not saying all your decisions will have the same effect, but if some of the most successful people to have ever lived do it, it should be enough for us to at least give it a try. Remember, success leaves clues.

In my own life, I've attempted to make things as routine and systemised as possible. Each day I wake up at 3:50 am. I walk the *same* way to the *same* twenty-four-hour café, order the *same* coffee, sit on the *same* side of the *same* table, take the *same* picture for my social feed, put my headphones in and listen to the *same* song for the next two hours while I write. At 6:10 am (as my laptop battery hits 8%) I pack up and head home - *of course walking the same way.* I then stretch while listening to a daily meditation to relax the mind. By 6:30 am it's time to walk my dog, where I walk the *same* way while listening to an audio book. After around an hour, I make my way home to eat the *same* breakfast, before getting into the day at 8:00 am. This is my life five days a week. Weekends vary slightly, but most of the time, this is how I like to live my life. Very routine, very 'boring', but it's this exact routine that allows me to achieve maximum output. The less variability the better. As we continue, have a think about what routines you can put in place to remove the variability in your life and systemise your energy.

Rituals Explained

Alone, though, Routines are not enough. While they will help you sustain battery power, we need to look at the second 'R' for recharging that battery. This makes up part two below on 'Rituals'.

Rituals aid in the speed at which you can recover. Rituals are all about 'you' time. A time to work on personal growth and energy renewal. As I mentioned earlier, each morning I adhere to my morning pages routine to clear my mind and download my thoughts. I also love getting a massage each week to release and relax my muscles, which I imagine as removing the toxins and tightness I've built up over the week while allowing my body to function at its highest level. I then love having monthly growth dinners with exceptional people (mentors, good friends) to expand my mind, thinking capacity and outlook on the world. Every time I have a growth dinner I walk away feeling inspired, energised and invigorated. In your own life, what Routines and Rituals do you currently adhere to? If you don't know, I have something that may help.

Getting Practical

What I have outlined for you below are some practical insights into each of our four energy systems. I have also included the consequences of inadequate recovery for each. Below that, I share some simple Routines and Rituals you might like to implement to ensure your stress and renewal practices are working together.

Physical Energy - The Body
What happens?   Without appropriate physical recovery, we are constantly tired and burnt-out.
What to do about it?   *Physical:*   - Two strength sessions + two high-intensity interval sessions per week. Movement every day.   *Nutrition:*   - Smaller, regular meals. More whole foods. Less processed food.   *Sleep:*   - Six-eight hours in a dark, interruption-free environment. Consistent wake-up and bedtime.   *Rest:*   - Brief but regular rest periods. Must switch attention from work.   - No eating in work environment.

Emotional Energy - Energy Quality
What happens? Without appropriate emotional recovery, we cannot make smart decisions.
What to do about it? - At intervals throughout the day, focus on deep breathing and mindful self-care. - When upset, put yourself in others' shoes and ask *How would I (re)act if this were me?*

Mental Energy - Focus of Energy
What happens? Without appropriate mental recovery, we cannot focus on what is most important to us.
What to do about it? - Focus in Fifty-four minute work blocks. Fifty-four minutes working distraction free (on), six minutes to have a break (off) - and then repeat. Fifty-four on, six off. Take a short 15 to 20 minute break, and repeat cycle again. - Set a timer and put phone on aeroplane mode if you can. - Batch tasks. Keep mundane tasks to later in the day when energy doesn't need to be at peak (ie, never check email first thing in morning). - Set your priorities early / night before.

Spiritual Energy - Meaning & Purpose
What happens?   Without appropriate spiritual recovery, we lose our desire to achieve, and lack purpose.
What to do about it?   - Do what you do best and enjoy most. Always think *How can I do more of what I love, and less of what I don't?*   - Ask yourself *When did I last feel inspired? What was I doing and how can I reverse engineer my life to do more of that and less of the draining tasks?*   - Spend focused, present time with family/friends and on things you like.   - Perform tasks that are aligned with your core values.

Putting it all together

Now that you're equipped with some sample Routines and Rituals necessary to renew and refresh your energy, let's look at putting it all together. Not only do most not have a plan to recharge and renew, but most are walking around like zombies and wondering why they can't get anything done. They run at a million miles per hour without taking the time necessary to stop and see where they could improve.

To reach peak performance in your life and fully step into leadership, you'll need two things. The first is to discover your ideal outcome. The second is to integrate Routines and Rituals around that outcome to help make success seamless.

We can call this our 'Success System'. Once we have this system in place, all that is required is to simply 'do the work' (the part most people don't want to do). The more you work the system, the more efficient and effective you'll become.

You need to discover where you're leaking energy and create your system to ensure you can perform at your best not just in the next one, two or five years, but every day for the rest of your life. Anyone can work themselves into the ground over a 12-month period and burn everything else around them in the process, but to truly build a life that creates impact and inspires others, you need to ensure longevity. The fewer holes in the bucket, the higher the output. Have a think about where you're leaking energy and what you're doing to renew it. Chances are, if you're feeling off, it's linked to the above. Effective leaders manage their lives by first managing their energy.

Now What?

By this stage, I am hoping you're feeling inspired and ready to take life on as the Young Leader you were destined to be.

And while many claim leaders are born, not bred, I can 100% tell you this is not the case. How do I know this? Because I've done it. I'm no different to you. I just made a decision one day that I no longer wanted to play small.

I decided I wanted to write a book. I decided I wanted to speak to the best minds on the planet and discover what makes them great. I decided I wanted to live each day with passion and commitment to a cause greater than myself. Now I want you to do the same. The question is, when will you start? Remember, the best time to plant a tree was 20 years ago; the second-best time is now.

Where to Start?

Ready to lead, but no idea who to lead or where to start? Start with these three questions:

1. What skills, knowledge, experience and expertise do I have that no-one else in the world has? (Refer back to your story for inspiration).

2. What do I see as 'wrong' with the world and what can I do to fix that?

3. What would need to happen for me to assemble a team of like-minded individuals who could help me achieve that goal faster?

This is the beginning of your tribe. Your movement. This is what leadership is all about. Inspire through action and watch what happens.

Feeling stuck?

At times we all get stuck. In fact, you'll find it refreshing to know that while on the surface, some of your biggest heroes might seem to have it all together, truth is quite often they don't.

Yes, you're reading a book I put together, but do you know how many times I doubted myself in the process? Not only has this taken much longer than I would have liked, but it's actually the fourth book I have attempted to put together. The thing is, no matter what you might think or see, everyone has fears, everyone has insecurities, everyone has self-doubt, everyone has worries, everyone feels guilt, everyone feels shame. No-one gets off scot-free. It's called being human. Welcome to the club - there's like 7 billion of us.

So many people feel they're alone on this journey, and, despite right now being the most connected society we've ever been, isn't it true we are also feeling increasingly isolated? We hide our fears from others to appear brave. We attempt to keep our self-doubt locked within the confines of our mind so as not to bother anyone in an attempt to cover our insecurities. We put on an empty smile and positive attitude, and for what?

Instead, I want to open the conversation. I invite you to reach out in times of need. Speak to a mentor, connect with a friend, get out and do something bigger than yourself. You are not alone. Of the billions of species on this earth of ours, humans are the only creatures capable of thinking about thinking. This can be a blessing or a burden, depending on which way you look at it. Don't hide in the darkness. Instead, open up and allow light to enter. You'll be glad you did.

The deathbed

Before I part with you, I want to share one final thing. Unless you've experienced a near death experience yourself, or been awoken to the realities of death in another form, you may believe there is infinite time. So many of us have a skewed perception of time. Most complain they don't have enough of it, yet they squander what they're given.

Ask yourself the following:

If I only had one year left to live, what would I do?

If I only had one month left to live, what would I do?

If I only had one week left to live, what would I do?

If I only had one day left to live, what would I do?

If I only had one hour left to live, what would I do?

If I only had one minute left to live, what would I do?

I believe at the end of our lives, on our deathbed, we'll ask the question of ourselves; *Did I do everything I could, with everything I had?* Best to make sure the answer is a definite yes.

Here's the thing - I may not know you; nor do I know the struggles you've faced throughout this life of yours. But one thing I do know is that your future can be bigger than your past. There is no time like now. Let the past be the past and let's focus on your future. Don't waste the remaining days of your life wondering what could have been. Instead, create your own reality.

In a world full of excuses, complaints and reasons not to, be bold and do it anyway. While most are claiming they're too old, too young, not experienced enough, not good enough, don't have the right skills, don't have the right connections, the timing isn't right, they need to ask their partner and every other excuse they can think of, be the change you wish to see in the world. Don't be a dreamer, be a do-er. You can either let your excuses win or you can take control of your life.

Young Leaders need to be prepared to offer the same level of excellence as the best in the world. Can you commit to that? Not many can, but there is room for some to achieve a huge level of success. So I have to ask, after reading this book...will it be you? I genuinely hope so.

Final Thoughts...

I believe everyone has a story to tell and everyone is worthy of having it reach the world. Me. You. Anyone. We all have the power to share what's in our heart, and once you make the decision that that's what you want, nothing can get in your way. The doubts, obstacles and challenges all become part of the journey. Instead of backing down, you suit up and prepare for battle.

How many times do we get told we *can't* do something as opposed to being told we can? How many stories go unwritten because of the doubters? Businesses that never get off the ground? Brilliant ideas that fall by the wayside because someone is selfish enough to shoot someone's dream down?

It doesn't have to be this way. One person at a time, we can change this. If we were to each champion at least one person around us and drag them up, instead of cutting them down, together we can create a wave of inspiration that will literally change the world.

And why can't you be part of that? Why can't you write a book? Start a business around what you love? Or tackle that next project?

Why wait to be great when you already are? The time is now. Be bold, take risks and lead the way. Don't ever let anyone tell you you can't, because I'm living proof you can. Time to show up, stand out and shine bright.....and go.

Thank you

I hope reading this book has inspired you as much as it has inspired me while writing it. Each morning I wake up and ask myself, *what can I do today to inspire others, bring more love into the world and do more of what I love? What can I write? What can I produce? What can I create?* I've developed a deep hunger to serve others, and my purpose is to inspire others through action.

If you're inspired and ready to take massive action, I'd love to hear from you. You can reach me directly at: hayden@haydenwilson.com.au or jump over to my website (haydenwilson.com.au) and discover the programmes I run to help Young Leaders show up, stand out and shine bright.

Thank-you again for taking the time to read this book. I look forward to serving you again soon.

About the Author

Hayden Wilson is an engaging Young Leader who lives to learn, share and grow in all areas of his life. His core philosophy is to inspire through action which helps drive new and innovative growth for those he teaches. He is the creator of many inspirational events, leadership development programmes and small coaching groups, all designed to help Young Leaders around the world show up, stand out and shine bright.

He is also the author of the book *Why Wait To Be Great*, an inspirational guide to help Young Leaders develop within their lives. He frequently travels internationally to learn from the world's best and uses this knowledge to build upon his proven techniques and methodologies learned from years of dedication to his craft. He hosts a popular podcast for Young Leaders which has seen him interview over a hundred experts in the fitness, health and leadership fields, as well as being the founder of *be nice.* - an international movement focused on sharing more 'nice' around the world.

Originally from Shepparton, Victoria, Hayden started from humble beginnings. From cleaning the floor of the fruit canning factory, SPCA, he now shares his love of learning with those dedicated to continuous development and obtaining more love in their lives.

Hayden looks forward to helping you achieve more inside your life than you previously thought possible. You can find out more about his programmes, hire him to speak at your next event or discuss how he can help you via his website: http://haydenwilson.com.au/

www.ingramcontent.com/pod-product-compliance
Lightning Source LLC
LaVergne TN
LVHW051348080426
835509LV00020BA/3337